Welcome to
Japanese

A Beginner's Survey of the Language

by Kenneth Henshall with Junji Kawai

TUTTLE PUBLISHING
Boston • Rutland, Vermont • Tokyo

Published by Tuttle Publishing, an imprint of Periplus Editions, with editorial offices at 153 Milk Street, Boston, Massachusetts 02109 and 130 Joo Seng Road #06-01/03, Singapore 368357.

Library of Congress Control Number: 2003112844
ISBN 0-8048-3376-1

First Edition 2004

Printed in Singapore

Distributors

North America, Latin America & Europe
Tuttle Publishing
364 Innovation Drive
North Clarendon, VT 05759-9436, USA
Tel: (802) 773 8930 Fax: (802) 773 6993
www.tuttlepublishing.com
Email: info@tuttlepublishing.com

Japan
Tuttle Publishing
Yaekari Building, 3F
5-4-12 Osaki, Shinagawa-ku
Tokyo 141 0032, Japan
Tel: (03) 5437 0171 Fax: (03) 5437 0755
Email: tuttle-sales@gol.com

Asia Pacific
Berkeley Books Pte Ltd
130 Joo Seng Road #06-01/03
Singapore 368357
Tel: (65) 6280 1330 Fax: (65) 6280 6290
Email: inquiries@periplus.com.sg

CONTENTS

Introduction

PART ONE   AN OVERVIEW OF THE JAPANESE LANGUAGE

Chapter 1: Getting Acquainted with the Language

Chapter 2: Challenges and Rewards

PART TWO   THE BUILDING BLOCKS: SOUNDS INTO WORDS

Chapter 3: Making the Right Noises

Chapter 4: It's Only Words?

PART THREE   WORDS INTO SENTENCES

Chapter 5: The Basic Parts of Speech

Chapter 6: More Advanced Usage

PART FOUR   SENTENCES INTO SCRIPT

Chapter 7: The Writing System

Afterword

Introduction

Welcome to *Welcome to Japanese*!

We emphasize the word "welcome" deliberately because we want readers to feel "at home" and "at ease." This book is aimed primarily at native English speakers, and because Japanese is a very different language from English and from the typical foreign language that English speakers might be familiar with, such as French or German, it is important that you do not feel alienated, intimidated or stressed. Rather, we want you to enjoy learning about the Japanese language.

Japanese has too often been treated by Westerners as an exotic curiosity, but the reality is that it is a functional language spoken as a mother tongue by more than 125 million people, and ranks as the ninth most spoken language in the world. In the present global age, an age characterized by a vast range of Japanese products including electronic games and anime, more and more Westerners are in one way or another interacting with Japan and its people. But it is nonetheless fair to say that the language, while increasing in popularity as a subject of study, is still not as widely spoken among non-Japanese as we might expect.

In this book we would therefore like to "demystify" Japanese, to show how the language is formed and used, and to encourage you to pursue the study of it. Of course it has its challenges, especially with regard to the writing system, but we try to put these in a balanced context. And we like to think that, by describing the various facets of the language to you, we thereby empower you with a degree of knowledge and familiarity.

Welcome to Japanese is not intended as a language learning textbook. Rather, it is an introductory description, comprising four parts: an overview; an account of how sounds are made into words; an account of how words are made into sentences; and finally an account of how the language is written.

Naturally, in the course of these accounts we will introduce a range of vocabulary, grammar and script, which will be useful in a learning context. In fact, for those interested, we go to fairly advanced levels in the description of grammar. We give you example sentences for each grammar point, and try to make our description as clear as possible, but we stress again that we do not intend this as a teaching text. There are no exercises, for instance, and it's very much a case of going through at your own pace and dwelling on those parts that you find most interesting.

However, having said that, we hope that those readers who wish to go on to study the language will find *Welcome to Japanese* a handy reference guide. For those who do not wish to pursue study of the language, reading this book will offer a basic understanding of the Japanese language to the satisfaction of one's curiosity.

Because we see this book as a platform for further learning, we have deliberately inclined to polite speech rather than the informal, though not to the point of pedantry and certainly not to the point where it might be deemed "old-fashioned" or "unnatural." Informal language can all too easily become slang, and that is not a good basis for learning a language. This is especially so in a "politeness-sensitive" culture such as Japan's. Hence you will see that, for example, we use people's names wherever possible rather than the pronouns **kare** and **kanojo** for "he" and "she," since, contrary to the impression created by some conversation books, these pronouns are not universally used, and can at times be considered quite vulgar and inappropriate.

This is about as dogmatic as we get. *Welcome to Japanese* is not cluttered with esoteric references or arcane arguments but is about a living language. We hope readers will enjoy discovering Japanese at their own pace, and finding out a range of interesting things that will even make them reflect on their own mother tongue and language in general (one reason we make frequent comparisons between Japanese and English and occasionally other languages). And we have tried to be "reader-friendly," choosing interesting examples where possible and even trying to inject the odd bit of humor.

After all, a language is not just something you learn in a classroom. It's a major tool in interpersonal communication, and the easier that is, the better.

In the preparation of this book we have been invaluably assisted by a number of people, including in particular Flavia Hodges, Adam Lam, and Neil Chandler. Our grateful thanks to them. But our biggest thanks go to those of you who read this book and decide that yes, Japanese is "do-able," and that you can have fun in the doing of it.

PART ONE

An Overview of the Japanese Language

In this part we give a brief introduction of the main distinguishing characteristics of the Japanese language. We then tell you who speaks and studies it, outline its origins and development, and go on to discuss what might be considered its challenges on the one hand and its rewards and less challenging aspects on the other.

CHAPTER ONE

Getting Acquainted with the Language

In this first chapter we profile the Japanese language to give you a basic "feel" for it. We show you how it compares with other languages, particularly English, and cover basic background such as its history and usage.

1.1 In a nutshell, what English speakers can expect

We will look later in detail at the various components of the Japanese language. But let us start off by considering in brief, and in comparative terms, some of the main features of the language as they generally strike a native English speaker. We will focus on four key areas—words, writing, grammar and usage.

1.1.1 Vocabulary

A reasonably well-educated native speaker of English will be familiar with around 25,000 words, and be able to use about two-thirds of those actively—though in typical everyday speech only around 3,000 are used.

Figures are roughly comparable for native speakers of Japanese, though they are higher by perhaps 15% or so. In general, Japanese also make a greater distinction between words actively used and those considered "bookish."

English is one of the world's richest languages, thanks to its diverse sources. The two principal sources are Romance (derived from Latin, often through French), and Germanic (including Anglo-Saxon and Scandinavian). In addition we have many words from ancient Greek and numerous other sources as varied as Czech ("robot") and Arabic ("algebra"), as well as those considered ancient native such as Celtic ("crag"). In conversation around three-quarters of the words we use are Anglo-Saxon.

Japanese also has diverse sources. In addition to a good stock of native words, comprising almost half of all its modern vocabulary, it has a similar proportion of its words coming from Chinese, and in modern times almost ten percent of its words derive from English. Chinese plays a similar role in Japanese as Romance words in English, and in particular often has associations with classicism and learning similar to Latin and Greek. As in English, Japanese also contains a number of modified words from a variety of other languages, such as Portuguese (**pan** for "bread," from *pão*), and German (**arubaito** for "part-time job," from *Arbeit*).

FIGURE 1a: Japanese vocabulary composition

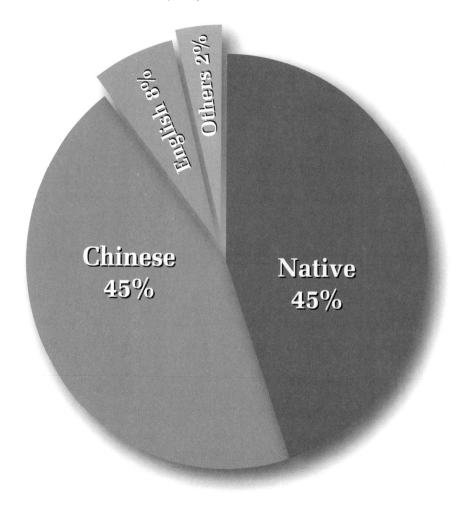

1.1.2 Writing system

The English script uses the Roman alphabet of 26 symbols, effectively doubled to allow for both upper and lower case. These are used phonetically, that is to say for their sound rather than any pictorial meaning. This seems very simple. There is however a huge range in the variety of pronunciations possible for these symbols, especially in combination—e.g. at least eight different ways of pronouncing "-ough" (in British English), such as in "thorough," "through," "though," "thought," "cough," "enough," "hiccough," and "bough." English spelling is among the most difficult in the world, and can be very daunting to a learner.

FIGURE 1b: Can you read this?

George Bernard Shaw is credited with illustrating the difficulty of English spelling by coming up with this spelling of a common word. What word do you think it is?

Clue: "gh" as in "enough," "o" as in "women," "ti" as in "station."

Second clue: yes, it swims in the sea!

Japanese, by contrast, can involve four different scripts. It can occasionally be written in the Roman alphabet (known as romaji), such as in textbooks or other material for foreigners or in certain advertising, but generally uses two phonetic scripts based on syllables (hiragana and katakana, collectively known as kana) in combination with characters derived from Chinese (known as kanji). Whereas phonetic scripts are based on sound, characters are based primarily on pictures or ideas, though confusingly they can in many cases also have phonetic elements and multiple pronunciations. It is this relatively complex and unfamiliar writing system, not the spoken language, that provides the major challenge for Westerners in learning Japanese to any truly advanced level.

1.1.3 Grammar

There are a number of significant differences between English and Japanese grammar—that is, the rules of language.

Whereas English is a Subject-Verb-Object (SVO) language ("the dog bit the boy"), Japanese is Subject-Object-Verb (SOV) ("dog boy bit"). In terms of the world's languages, there are approximately equal numbers in both categories, so it cannot be said that Japanese is unusual in this regard.

English usually relies on word-order or sometimes change of word-form to distinguish subject and object (e.g. "he" is the subject, "him" is the object), but Japanese primarily uses particles to do this. A particle is a short word (such as **wa**, **ga** or **o**) that is not always translatable in itself but is used as a sort of suffix to indicate the grammatical role of the word it follows. Among other things particles can convey similar meaning to that produced in English by articles such as "the" or "a," which do not exist as such in Japanese. English has articles, Japanese has particles.

Other differences the English speaker will encounter include greater conceptual and grammatical overlap between verbs and adjectives, the frequent omission of pronouns, the frequent omission of indication of plurality or singularity, the absence of verb conjugation according to person (restricted in English relative to, say, French, but still found in "I see, she see**s**" and the verb "to be"), the absence of a dedicated future-only tense, the structure of subordinate clauses, and a greater sensitivity to politeness. Many of these differences boil down to Japanese generally being less explicit and specific than English.

TABLE 1a: Key grammatical differences between Japanese and English

ENGLISH	JAPANESE
subject-verb-object	subject-object-verb
articles (a, the)	particles (**ga**, **wa**)
some verb change according to person/number	no verb change according to person/number
dedicated future tense	no dedicated future tense
pronouns almost always used	pronouns often omitted
relative clauses follow item	relative clauses precede item
pronouns show subj./obj. (he/him)	pronouns unchanged
not especially politeness-sensitive	very politeness-sensitive
frequent explicitness	frequent implicitness

1.1.4 Socio-cultural context

To a considerable extent languages reflect the cultures in which they are embedded, and in turn the particular worldview and ordering of life characteristic of that culture. In other words, as many theorists argue, your language helps shape the way you interpret the world. If there is a significant dislocation between your first language and the surrounding culture in which you find yourself, feelings of alienation can arise, as can happen with immigrants or travelers. And because both culture and language are dynamic, this feeling of alienation can even occur in your native country—the generation gap is such an example.

Since Japanese culture is markedly different in many regards from English (or Anglo) culture, this will be reflected in language usage. What is "right" is often a matter of convention, or what anthropologists call ritual. All languages have ritualized elements, which have a socio-cultural meaning beyond or different from their literal meaning. For example, are you really enquiring about a person's state of health when you greet them with "How are you?" Similarly, when Japanese meet early in the morning (before around 10 a.m.) they will say **Ohayō gozaimasu** meaning literally "It's early." (We will discuss the letter **ō** in Part Two.) They do not expect a reply such as "Thank you for letting me know. I hadn't realized." Such a reply would almost certainly be deemed grossly sarcastic.

In terms of degree the Japanese language is considerably ritualized. In a given situation, the balance between the obligation to use conventionalized language, and the freedom to do or say "your own thing," is more likely to incline to the former than an English speaker might expect.

The English speaker will also note in particular that despite substantial recent socio-cultural changes Japanese is still a significantly rank-oriented and gender-differentiated language. References to the self often differ from the English. So do insults and metaphors. For example, insults and oaths involving references to private parts of the body or religious icons and so forth do not necessarily carry any weight in Japanese, where good old-fashioned idiocy is the main theme of insults.

Basically, word associations, language usages and conventions that may be broadly shared within the Anglophone world, and indeed more broadly much of the West, are not necessarily the same in Japan.

1.2 Who speaks Japanese?

We look here at the native speakers of Japanese, and those who learn it as a second or other language.

1.2.1 Native speakers

Japanese is obviously spoken by native Japanese in Japan, who comprise some 98% of the 127 million Japanese-speaking population. In addition, it is spoken (or maintained) as a "heritage language" by more than a million people from Japanese emigrant families, notably in areas with a significant ethnic Japanese population such as Hawaii, parts of California and, to a lesser extent, certain parts of South America. Many children of Korean and Chinese immigrants in Japan also speak Japanese as their first language even though they may not be Japanese citizens.

In total, roughly 125–130 million people speak Japanese as a mother tongue or close to it. This contrasts with the approximately 835 million native speakers of Mandarin Chinese (the language with the most native speakers), and 325 million or so native speakers of variants of English (the most widely spoken language).

Though it is not designated as one of the United Nations' six official languages (in alphabetical order: Arabic, Chinese, English, French, Russian and Spanish), it ranks ninth in the world in terms of the number of native speakers (after Mandarin Chinese, Hindi, Spanish, English, Bengali, Arabic, Russian, and Portuguese).

Japanese is also becoming increasingly prominent as an internet language.

FIGURE 1c: "Top Ten" languages (in millions of speakers)

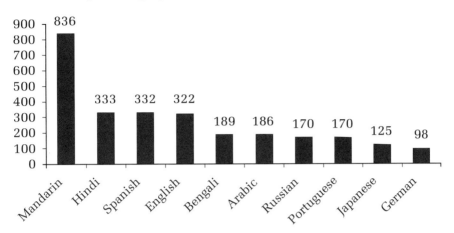

1.2.2 Non-native speakers and students

Those who study Japanese as a Second or Other Language are some-times referred to as JSOL speakers.

Partly due to Japan's prominence as an economic superpower Japanese is now studied widely around the world—though admittedly not to the same degree as English, which has become a truly international lan-guage with more than a billion non-native students. At any given time there are about 2 million people studying Japanese, with a general rate of increase of around 5% per year. As many as 100,000 students, mainly from Asia, go to Japan each year for language study in one form or an-other. And in countries with significant geo-political as well as eco-nomic links with Japan, Japanese is studied extensively, both privately and at educational institutions. South Korea tops the list of (current) formal students of Japanese as a percentage of overall population, with just over 2%, followed by Australia and New Zealand, both around 1.5% (as opposed to the USA's 0.04% and Britain's 0.02%). In recent years Japanese has displaced French in Australia and New Zealand as the most popular foreign language chosen by school students.

FIGURE 1d: Select population percentages studying Japanese

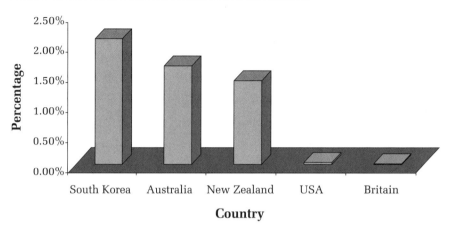

Japanese was spoken as a second—or even technically as a "first"—language by Koreans and some Chinese who experienced Japanese occupation prior to 1945, and for whom use of the Japanese language was compulsory. However, it is not actively used by those people today in those countries.

1.3 Where did the Japanese language come from?

We consider here how the Japanese language came to be what it is now. Along the way we consider questions such as "Is it unique?", "Who first spoke it?", "Has it changed much over time?", and "Is it standardized?"

1.3.1 Where does it belong?

Japanese has defied attempts by scholars of linguistics to place it with any certainty in any one language family. That is, unlike the vast majority of the world's languages, it belongs in a category of its own. This contrasts with English, which, like most European (and Indian) languages, derives from an ancient Indo-European core language. To be precise, English quite demonstrably belongs to the Anglo-Frisian branch of the West Germanic group within the Indo-European family.

The closest language neighbor of Japanese is Korean, which has considerable grammatical similarities. Korean is loosely placed in the Altaic family (along with Turkish and Mongolian), but this is questionable, and any placement of Japanese in the Altaic family even more so. Japanese also shows some evidence, especially in sound structure, of lesser links with the Austronesian language family of the Southwest Pacific, such as the Maori language in New Zealand.

FIGURE 1e: Simplified language families

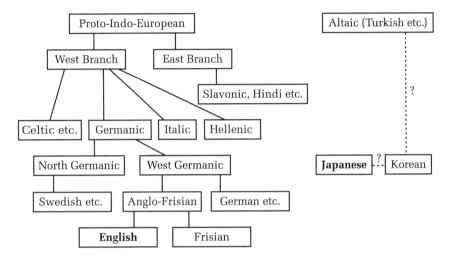

1.3.2 What are its origins?

The origins of the Japanese language, like the origins of the Japanese people, are not entirely clear. Until around 2,500 years ago the Japanese islands were principally inhabited by groups of basically related peoples now referred to collectively as the Jōmon. Over the next thousand years waves of immigrants arrived, largely through the Korean Peninsula, and displaced (in some cases intermixing with) the Jōmon. These newcomers—who were basically related among themselves, but significantly differed from the Jōmon—were later called Yayoi people, or more generally Yamato people. They constitute more than 99% of present-day native Japanese. Physical links with the Jōmon are found in the indigenous Ainu of Japan's northern island of Hokkaido, of whom about 20,000 survive. So the Ainu language might in a historical sense be considered the first identifiable language of Japan, or at least a direct descendant of it (just as the Celtic language Erse, now spoken only in a few parts of Scotland, might be considered the first identifiable language of Britain). However, it is even more difficult to associate Ainu with any language family than Japanese as we know it today, which is the Japanese of the immigrant Yamato people.

Certainly, however, the obscure and now almost extinct oral tongue of the Ainu (Jōmon?) will have had some impact on the early development of Japanese, for the Yamato newcomers absorbed at least some of its vocabulary. The name of Japan's famous volcano Mount Fuji, for example, is believed to be derived from an Ainu word *fuchi*, meaning "Fire God." And in fact the Japanese word *kami*, meaning "a (Shinto) god," almost certainly comes from the Ainu *kamui*, meaning "a god" (and not vice versa, as some Japanese linguists claim).

1.3.3 How has it developed over time?

Like English, the Japanese language—that is, the language of the Yamato people—has changed markedly over the centuries. Old Japanese had more sounds (e.g. eight vowels as opposed to the present five), and was much more inflected (having numerous changes to word-endings), in particular producing complicated combinations of verb tenses.

It existed as a purely spoken language till around the fifth century, when Chinese script, which was developed for a very different type of language, was borrowed as a supposedly "ready-made" means of writing Japanese. The consequences of this questionable move will be discussed in more detail later, but it can be noted here that although characters were adopted principally for their meaning, and pronounced as the equivalent-meaning Japanese spoken word, they also had Chinese pronunciations of their own, which also entered the Japanese language (with considerable modification in some cases). Other characters were borrowed specifically for their pronunciation in order to express Japanese words or word-elements in writing. Also, many Chinese words (especially compounds) were adopted. And so, especially from around the seventh and eighth centuries, Japanese became considerably "Sinified."

Presently, kana phonetic symbols were produced from certain characters used primarily for their sound rather than meaning, and were initially applied (in the case of katakana) as pronunciation guides to characters. Eventually kana were also used for writing native Japanese words, especially the more cursive hiragana, which were used largely by women. Among other things this meant that Japanese people could now write in a way that Chinese people could not readily understand (that is, not without study).

Westerners first arrived in Japan in 1543, and stayed for around a century before being expelled. They were mostly Portuguese, and later Dutch (who alone among Westerners avoided total expulsion and were allowed a small settlement), and these two nations left a legacy of a number of words that were incorporated into Japanese. However, it was when the Westerners returned in 1853, this time for good, that Japanese underwent its next major change. This time it was English that was the major influence. In fact, as Japan set out on its course of modernization—which to a large extent meant Westernization—there was even a move among certain people in high places to adopt English as the official language. This move, in similar fashion to the eighteenth century proposal to make German the official language of the United States, was taken seriously and only narrowly failed to gain acceptance. Had it not failed, you would now be studying Japanese as an archaic language, not as a living one!

FIGURE 1f: What might have been...

During the decades following the return of the Westerners, in addition to numerous new words adopted from English and other Western languages there were many new Sino-Japanese words coined, such as for "telegraph" and presently "automobile." A similar process occurred in China at around the same time, and there was borrowing both ways between China and Japan so it is not always clear in which country particular words were coined. There was also a brief revival of very heavily Sinified language among scholars, and a reasonably successful attempt by novelists to bridge what was up until then a substantial gap between spoken and written language styles. In recognition of the complexity of the writing system, there was also a proposal to abandon kanji and use only kana, but, like the move to adopt English, this ended up failing to gain acceptance.

During the strong nationalistic atmosphere leading up to World War Two, there was a move to ban Western words and replace them with Japanese (or Sino-Japanese) words. This had limited success in practice, and, following Japan's defeat and the largely American occupation that ensued, the profile of English in Japan and in the Japanese language greatly increased. As we shall see later, the Japanese are now actually making up their own "English" terms and phrases, known as "Japlish," and in some cases re-exporting them to the English-speaking world!

As internationalization and globalization progress, changes to languages worldwide are inevitable. Given the Japanese ability to adapt and modify, we can expect that the language will evolve into an even more hybrid form, despite the significant degree of ritual language use mentioned earlier.

1.3.4 What is "standard" Japanese?

The standard language that now represents (British) English is often referred to—somewhat inaccurately—as the "Queen's English." However, the Japanese monarch's title has never been seen as a representation of standard Japanese, for the language of the Imperial Household, though now less distinct than in the past—very few members of the public could understand Emperor Hirohito's surrender speech when the first imperial radio broadcast was made in August 1945—is still not very representative of ordinary Japanese. Rather, standard Japanese might be termed, like "BBC English," to be "NHK Japanese," based on the language of the nation's principal broadcaster Nihon Hōsō Kyoku (Japan Broadcasting Corporation). This in turn is based largely on the dialect of the capital, Tokyo.

There are many rich and varied dialects in Japan, more so than in England, but in this book we focus on standard "NHK Japanese."

CHAPTER TWO

Challenges and Rewards

Every language has, for the learner from another language background, what might be termed "good news" and "not quite so good news." Japanese is no exception. In this chapter, from an English speaker's perspective, we consider the straight-out good news first, in Section 2.1. Then in 2.2 we introduce you to the challenges, but soften these by giving you tips along the way so as to reduce the level of challenge. That's why we refer to it as "not quite so good news" rather than simply "bad news."

All points raised in this chapter will be discussed in more detail later in the book, so don't worry if you are left wanting more information on some particular point.

2.1 The good news
We shall consider here different types of "good news." These are the rewards of learning Japanese, and the downright "easy bits."

2.1.1 The rewards
Although Japanese does have its challenges, it is almost always seen as rewarding, even by those who do not pursue their studies beyond an introductory level. These rewards are both material and personal.

Japan is one of the world's major nations. Even though its economy has been relatively unhealthy for more than a decade now, it is not going to cease being a world superpower. And yet, despite increasing numbers of native English speakers becoming competent in Japanese, especially proportionately in countries such as Australia and New Zealand, worldwide these are still few relative to those competent in the traditional foreign languages of French and German. That is, Westerners competent in Japanese have a very useful rarity, and possess a skill much in demand. (Having said that, the growth of students of Japanese mentioned earlier may eventually erode that rarity value.)

A recent UK survey revealed that more and more young Britons are keen to study Japanese because they love Japanese animé, and other surveys show that young Americans also think it is a "cool" language. This interest value is another significant factor, in that learning Japanese clearly satisfies a personal interest for many students, and is not merely a planned career decision. In terms of personal development and satisfaction, there is also great reward in the very learning of a language characterized by different concepts and cultural associations. Japan's culture, along with its history, is one of the richest in the world, and command of the language provides an extra dimension of accessibility to it. And in terms of broadening the mind by learning another language, it follows that the more different from English that language is, the more the English speaker's mind will be broadened.

2.1.2 The easy bits

Some things about using Japanese—certainly in its spoken form—are downright easy. For example, you don't have to worry about gender of nouns or conjugating verbs according to person, or noun/pronoun changes depending on whether they are subject or object. And, compared with many languages, Japanese verbs do not contain many irregularities at all in terms of tense change.

English has become such a part of the linguistic consciousness of the Japanese that in many cases you can simply use English words and be understood. Even if a word has not formally entered the Japanese language, many Japanese would be familiar enough with the English vocabulary to understand it from the given context. (The Japanese grasp of English grammar is not quite so advanced, so whole English sentences and long phrases should be avoided.) This would be especially true if you put it into an appropriate Japanese sound structure—basically sequences of syllables comprising consonant plus vowel, as will be discussed in Part Two. But even if you didn't feel confident about "Japanizing" a word, there would be little misunderstanding, for example, if you just said "biscuit" instead of the properly Japanized word **bisuketto**. As an extra plus, the use of English terminology in Japanese can actually appear very stylish, just as using French in English seems a little chic and conveys a certain *je ne sais quoi*.

Japanese has fewer sounds to master than English, and there is no need to worry about stress or tones, as in Chinese. There is however a differentiation in pitch (making a sound high or low), which in particular can help distinguish between certain homophones (words with the same pronunciation) or near-homophones. Many students, especially in the past, have not worried about pitch at all, but it will help your accent and communicative efficiency greatly if you pay attention to it. We will return to this in Part Two.

In reading and writing too, at least in the kana scripts, the pronunciation and spelling of words are also much easier than in English, as there is a more consistent correspondence in Japanese between symbol and sound—not completely consistent, and not perhaps as straightforward as some languages such as French or Italian, but more so than in English.

There are many other pleasant surprises you will find along the way, when you discover that the particular aspect of Japanese that you are learning at a given time proves to be much easier than you expected.

2.2 The not quite so good news

Being in a language category of its own, it is not surprising that many of the more challenging aspects of Japanese can be attributed in large part to unfamiliarity—as foreshadowed earlier. In this section we look at the main features that most English speakers would consider challenging, but lessen the challenge by giving you advice along the way.

2.2.1 Japanese as "the Devil's language"

In the sixteenth century a certain Portuguese priest, one of the first-ever Westerners to visit Japan, became frustrated at his inability to master the language rapidly so as to spread God's word through it, and even termed it "the Devil's language."

It does indeed take time to become fully competent in all four skills of the language—listening, speaking, reading and writing, with the last two being very much more time-consuming. In fact, for native English speakers it takes about five times longer to achieve equivalent full competency in Japanese than in French, with its easier script and greater familiarity to English speakers. To start off your study without an awareness of this relativity can result in considerable frustration.

But let's put this into context. The skills of listening and speaking are by no means difficult to master in Japanese, though it is true you are disadvantaged to some extent if you can't reinforce verbal material by reading and writing it. But certainly, the spoken language is not quite so super-humanly inaccessible as our Portuguese friend suggests.

Its accessibility is borne out by (among other things) the increasing numbers of Japan-based Westerners who quite quickly become fluent in Japanese, even to the point of appearing as regulars on television quiz shows or similar conducted in Japanese. The Japanese word for a TV star is **tarento**, from the English word "talent." While these foreign personalities may be talented performers, they are not all abnormally talented linguists. Nevertheless, they have responded highly successfully to the challenge of spoken Japanese, showing clearly that it is very "do-able."

And as for the skills of reading and writing, individuals differ in their approach to learning Japanese. Some prefer to tackle the written language straightaway, which is the norm for most second languages. Others, mindful of the time-consuming nature of the writing system, concentrate first on the spoken language, to provide a sound base for later study of the written version—and of course, "later" can be anywhere between "just a bit later" and "so much later it's close to never." The "spoken first" approach is certainly how we learn our mother tongue, so it is by no means unnatural and ineffective. Unless your circumstances leave you no option, we suggest the obvious: choose whatever approach you feel most comfortable with.

FIGURE 2a: The Devil's language?

2.2.2 **The big written challenge**

Overwhelmingly the single biggest challenge for most Western students lies in the writing system. As you will see in detail in Part Four, it is one of the most complicated writing systems in the world. To read a newspaper you will need to know not only the two phonetic kana scripts of around 50 symbols each, but also around 2,000 kanji, each typically with two or three readings which may be based either on ancient Chinese or native Japanese, or in most cases both. It takes considerable time and gray matter to remember meanings and readings, and then on top of that, which readings are used in which circumstances.

This contrasts strongly with French, for example: native English speakers take a short time to learn correspondence patterns between spoken sound and Roman script, plus a few accent-signs, and they are able to read and write very quickly almost anything they speak or hear in that language.

As cold comfort for Western students, even Asian learners who are already familiar with Chinese characters are only partly advantaged by their prior knowledge. They are generally able to understand simple signs written in Japanese characters, such as for "Exit" or "No Smoking"; they can probably make an educated guess as to the basic gist of some formal Japanese texts heavy in characters, especially if there are lots of nouns (even though character forms nowadays often differ to some extent between Japanese and Chinese). However, for further understanding they would still have to learn the kana scripts, since the characters are used only for stems of words and not endings such as tenses, nor for particles. And they would also obviously have to learn the rules of grammar.

In addition, they would find the pronunciation different, even when it was meant to be a "Chinese" reading. For example, the characters for China, 中国, are in Chinese spelled *Zhongguo* and pronounced rather like *jong-guwo*, but in Japanese are spelled ***Chūgoku*** and pronounced *chew-gockoo*. (We will explain the letter *ū* in Part Two.)

Also, in some cases the same characters have evolved rather different meanings in each country, and likewise, some compounds do not necessarily have the same meaning in Chinese and Japanese. A classic example is 手紙, combining the characters for "hand" and "paper." In

Japanese this means "letter" (correspondence), but in Chinese means "toilet paper"! So, in some regards, prior knowledge of Chinese characters—or at least their Chinese pronunciations—might even be considered counter-productive.

FIGURE 2b: Now then, which one should I choose?

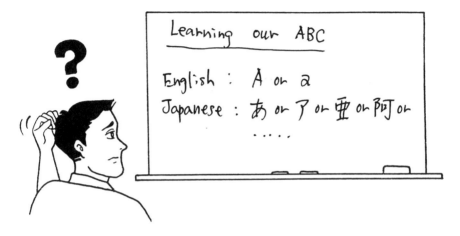

So, what can you do to lessen the challenge? First of all, as suggested in the previous section, you can postpone learning the writing system, maybe even indefinitely. This would mean that when it comes to having to write something in Japanese you would be stuck with romaji (or nothing). Most Japanese can manage to read romaji, if slowly, though few are really comfortable with it, so you would not be terribly popular.

A far better alternative is to communicate in the kana scripts (or even just one of these), which can be learned in just a few dozen hours or so as both kana scripts are based on the same sounds in the same sequence, comprise only a few strokes, and have only 46 basic symbols each.

An even better way, for those prepared to make the next step, is to learn a few basic kanji, such as the 80 that are taught in the First Grade at elementary school. These are generally quickly learned (again within a few dozen or so hours), easy to remember (many being simple pictographs), comprise only a few strokes, and are among the most commonly used. This means you will get maximum output of communicative ability relative to the input of time and effort. Unless you are a professional who requires a full command of the written language, few Japanese will think badly of you if you have only a very limited ability to write kanji. They too know the challenges involved! On the contrary, they will respect the fact that you have made an effort to communicate in something approaching proper written Japanese. Of course, when it comes to reading, you will still not be able to read newspapers, or indeed anything but Grade One elementary school texts! However, to get to that newspaper stage is a bit of a quantum leap, and everyone understands that.

If you want to go further, a good way is to concentrate on learning kanji passively rather than actively, that is, simply to recognize them rather than write them. Many students try to learn actively each kanji they encounter, which is a great strain on the memory cells, and they all too often end up after several years being able to recognize something like 1,000 and being able to write about 700 of those. It would be far better, after the same period of time spent studying, for you to be able to recognize all 2,000, even if you could only write a few hundred. The key thing is to understand what is put before you, and Japanese written material typically involves a liberal use of kanji, so you need to be able to know their meanings or at least be able to look them up quickly in a dictionary. You can use a smaller number of kanji, writing words in kana when you don't know the kanji for them.

And, when it comes to using a kanji dictionary, it will be much quicker if you can just make sure you remember at least one reading for each, since with modern dictionaries this will usually enable you to look up that kanji more quickly than trying to work out stroke count or radical component—a radical being the key element in a kanji, the traditional way of listing and searching for them. (Of course, this doesn't work for characters you encounter for the first time, unless you recognize a phonetic component.)

One plus about the kanji script is that, once you understand the core meanings, you can actually make fairly accurate guesses when you encounter new kanji compound words. This is not always the case with newly encountered words in English, unless you are familiar with Latin and Greek. Some advanced students even feel that speed-reading can be easier in Japanese than in English. For example, the meaning of the English word "glacier" is not immediately apparent to those encountering it for the first time, whereas the Japanese term **hyōga** involves the two kanji for "ice" and "river"—much easier to understand, provided you know the core kanji meanings.

2.2.3 The strangely worded challenge

The second major challenge is the lack of familiarity with much of the vocabulary, meaning that it is in that sense "strange" to the typical English speaker. If the English student of French or Spanish hears or sees the word *liberté* or *libertad* for the first time they would almost certainly understand this straightaway as "liberty," or similarly the German *frei* as "free." By contrast, the Japanese for both "liberty" and "free" is **jiyū**. That is, there is no clue for the English speaker.

Jiyū is actually a Chinese-derived word, one of many that have become an integral part of Japanese since the introduction of Chinese script many centuries ago. But pure Japanese words are no more helpful. For example, English cat-lovers would soon overcome language barriers in identifying a French *chat*, Spanish *gato*, or German *Katze*. They might need more time, however, to become familiar with a Japanese **neko**.

FIGURE 2c: Answer me a riddle

"I'm not a Spanish gato
Or an English cat.
I'm not a German Katze,
And not a French chat."

"What am I?
I'm a Japanese NEKO,
And I'm very proud of that!
— And I'm famous too!"*

*I am a Cat (**Wagahai wa neko de aru**) is one of Japan's best-known novels, written in 1905 by Natsume Sōseki. (**Wagahai** is an old word for "I"; **wa** is a subject-marker; **de aru** means "am.")

It is true that you don't have much control over the vocabulary the other party uses, though many Japanese people, recognizing the obvious fact that you are foreign, will often make a special effort to use loan words that they assume you will probably be familiar with. And certainly when it comes to speaking Japanese yourself, because Japanese has in recent times absorbed so many foreign words, especially English, you can use this very much to your advantage by using "Japanized English" should you forget or not know the "real" Japanese. For example, the "real" Japanese word for "book" is **hon**, but nowadays **bukku** can also be used. Likewise **miruku** for "milk" (as opposed to **gyūnyū**), **kā** for "car" (as opposed to **kuruma** or **jidōsha**), **konpyūta** for "computer," and so on. English words for material and/or technical objects are particularly common, though they are sometimes abbreviated. Thus "differential gear" is **difu-giya**. You do need to appreciate, however, that equivalents might not be exactly the same with some terms, with for example **miruku** and **gyūnyū** having slightly different usages (this will be discussed in Part Two), but at least your basic meaning will be understood.

And as mentioned in the section on "easy bits," as a worst-case scenario, just try using simple English. There's no need to shout, which is the typical English speaker's method of communicating with foreigners, but saying a word slowly and clearly will be helpful. Japanese people all learn English at school and often have a good passive knowledge of English words, though they may never have heard them actually articulated (at least by a native speaker).

2.2.4 The unspoken challenge

Another significant challenge lies in the grammar, which, like its vocabulary, is generally not familiar to native English speakers. As mentioned earlier this is seen in the word order, in the use of particles to indicate case (grammatical role), and in overlaps between adjectives and verbs (with adjectives being marked for tense as if they were verbs proper).

The grammar is generally less explicit and thus more vague and more potentially confusing than most Western languages. That is, more is left unsaid. For example, there is often no distinction made between singular and plural. Thus **neko** can mean "cat" or "cats." Verbs within a given tense do not conjugate according to person, as, for example, in English "I see, he sees," or even more so the French endings -e, -es, -e, -ons, -ez, -ent. Combined with the frequent omission of pronouns which indicate the subject of the verb, this can be particularly vague. And speaking of tenses, there is no dedicated future tense in Japanese, as the tense used is the same as the habitual present. Thus, **eiga** ("movie") **o** ("object particle") **mimasu** ("watch/see") can mean "I watch movies (as a regular thing)" or "I will watch a movie" or "somebody other than myself regularly watches movies or will watch a movie or multiple movies"!

Basically, though the language can certainly be specific and precise when necessary, in general Japanese is often implicit whereas Westerners are used to explicit language. That is, it is not what is spoken but often what is left unspoken that can be a challenge. Therefore the context becomes particularly important for inferring precise meaning, and this in itself can be challenging (as discussed in 1.1.4, on socio-cultural context).

But this "vague" grammar can actually be a plus depending on how you look at it. Unlike French and many other languages, when using Japanese you do not have to worry about the gender of nouns, the conjugation of verbs according to subject, or the formation of plurals. And, let's face it, sometimes it pays to be vague! How many times have you stuck your neck out to be specific about something only to regret it!

2.2.5 The challenge with a difference

There are numerous other particular points that will strike the English speaker as challenging simply because they are different and unfamiliar. For example, Japanese uses a wide range of different number-suffixes when counting, depending on the category of the item being counted. Thus **san-bon** means three long cylindrical objects, while **san-mai** means three thin flat objects, and so on. But is this any different in principle from the collective nouns in English—a "pride" of lions as opposed to a "pod" of dolphins?

Similarly, in English we say "I'm going out to post a letter", when in fact there are almost always not two but three actions involved: going, posting the letter, and returning. Perhaps we are not that bothered about the returning bit! The Japanese, by contrast, say "I'm posting a letter and coming back," and don't seem concerned about how they get to the postbox!

As a third example, replies to negative questions are also frequently different from English. In reply to a question "Aren't you going?" English speakers (if they were not going) would normally reply "No, I'm not." A Japanese, by contrast, would usually reply "Yes, I'm not" and this is even more confusing if the answer is just "Yes." The English-speaking respondent focuses on the action, which in this case is negative, whereas the Japanese respondent focuses on the accuracy or otherwise of the question, in effect using "yes" to indicate "You are correct." Which is the more valid as a reply? Of course, both are equally valid.

FIGURE 2d: How should I answer?

In the old days Western visitors to Japan often referred to it as a "topsy-turvy" land because so much of its language and culture seemed to be the opposite of what they were used to. But it works both ways; the Westerners and their ways and words seemed pretty weird to the Japanese in turn. In our present day we recognize that it's simply different ways of approaching the same thing.

There are many more examples such as this, where Japanese and English do not correspond exactly. The key thing is to keep an open mind, and to see differences as interesting challenges rather than difficult problems. The very fact that you are reading this book voluntarily (as opposed to being forced) shows that you are interested in learning Japanese, and so there is a very high probability that you are the sort of person who will respond positively to the challenge of difference.

You will probably also be able to work out your own "solutions" or "short cuts" when it comes to tricky aspects of the language. For example, you will probably have worked out for yourself that one way of avoiding a confusing response to a negative question you might be asked (such as "Aren't you going?") is to avoid saying **ee/hai** "yes" or **ie** "no" and simply give the substance (i.e. "I'm not going" or "I am going").

FIGURE 2e: Let's be pragmatic

As Japan's international profile increases, we are all becoming more familiar with Japanese culture and even with a number of Japanese words. You probably already know at least twenty Japanese words from the hundred or so that have entered English, such as **samurai**, **geisha** and **karate**. This helps reduce the aura of exoticism and "alienness" that underlies so many of the perceived challenges.

And the bottom line when it comes to challenges? The Japanese have shown by their technology and in many other ways that they are a very smart people, but like any group they too have their share of those who are not quite so smart. Yet they all manage, even the least bright and least motivated among them, to learn the language up to at least a functional level. (In fact, it is a basic law of linguistics that any established language must by definition be able to be adequately mastered by those who use it as a first language.) And, perhaps surprisingly, despite having one of the world's most complex scripts the Japanese also have the world's highest literacy rate, at over 98%! Of course they have more exposure to the language, but nevertheless, this reality-check goes to show that the challenge of Japanese is not insurmountable.

Let us now move on to Part Two, in which we start to look at Japanese in terms of the formation of sounds and words.

PART TWO

The Building Blocks: Sounds into Words

In this part of the book we look in detail at the basic components of the Japanese language so that you can start to see how it is made up. We cover sounds and words, before moving on to grammar in Part Three to show you how these words are actually used in sentences. Japanese script will be introduced in Part Four.

CHAPTER THREE

Making the Right Noises

Let us begin by looking at the sounds that make up the very basis of Japanese. This is one of the relatively "easy bits" referred to in Part One.

Good pronunciation symbolizes respect for a language, and that counts for a lot in Japan as in many countries. It is therefore important to make the right sounds.

Unfortunately, it is very difficult to convey correct pronunciation in a written text, certainly without resorting to technical phonetic symbols. One of the main problems is that English pronunciation can vary greatly between English-speaking nations, so that any example we gave for British readers might be very misleading for Americans, and vice versa.

We therefore strongly recommend that you take every possible opportunity to try out your spoken Japanese with native speakers, and similarly to use tapes, and listen to Japanese television programs if these are available to you.

3.1 The basic sound structure
The sound structure of Japanese is simpler than English, with fewer sounds and none of those awkward super-long syllables such as "strength" or "broached" or "sixths." In English there are also ambivalent syllables such as "clear" or "flower"—are these one syllable or two? Japanese does have a similar sort of ambivalence when it comes to certain syllables, although much of its sound system is composed of straightforward "consonant + vowel" combinations.

It is actually easier to think not so much in terms of syllables as of moras, a mora being a crisper, shorter unit of sound that can be thought of as a "beat."

Japanese has 101 basic moras (moraic sounds), these being the different sounds as set out in Tables 3a and 3b together (duplicated sounds are indicated by brackets). The consonants in 3b are "hardened" forms of some of the consonants in 3a, i.e. *g* being the hardened form of *k*, *z* and *j* hardened forms of *s* and sometimes *t*, *d* the hardened form of *t*, and *p* and *b* being semi-hardened and hardened forms of *h*. Learning this lay-out will help you greatly when it comes to tackling the kana writing system, which is syllabic (or more exactly, largely moraic) rather than based on individual letters as in English. We defer the actual kana symbols till Part Four.

TABLE 3a: Basic moraic sounds in Japanese

	A	I	U	E	O	-YA	-YU	-YO
Vowels	a	i	u	e	o			
K-	ka	ki	ku	ke	ko	kya	kyu	kyo
S-	sa	shi	su	se	so	sha	shu	sho
T-	ta	chi	tsu	te	to	cha	chu	cho
N-	na	ni	nu	ne	no	nya	nyu	nyo
H-	ha	hi	hu	he	ho	hya	hyu	hyo
M-	ma	mi	mu	me	mo	mya	myu	myo
Y-	ya		yu		yo			
R-	ra	ri	ru	re	ro	rya	ryu	ryo
W-	wa			(o)				
-N	-n							

TABLE 3b: Hardened moraic sounds in Japanese

	A	I	U	E	O	-YA	-YU	-YO
G-	ga	gi	gu	ge	go	gya	gyu	gyo
Z-/J-	za	ji	zu	ze	zo	ja	ju	jo
D-/J-	da	(ji)	(zu)	de	do	(ja)	(ju)	(jo)
P-	pa	pi	pu	pe	po	pya	pyu	pyo
B-	ba	bi	bu	be	bo	bya	byu	byo

It's important to note the following:

- All the sounds in these tables are stand-alone vowels, or consonant followed by vowel—in syllabic terms, "open syllables"—with the exception of *-n* (called the "moraic nasal"). The latter always follows a vowel and should not be confused with the *n-* row. It can never be used at the onset of a syllable, so it cannot start a word.

- Apparent irregularities such as *shi* instead of *si* result from modern Romanization systems that attempt to give a more accurate pronunciation guide to Western readers. That is, the Japanese *si* is actually closer to *shi*. (In earlier times it was indeed written *si*, and similarly *chi* and *tsu* were written *ti* and *tu* respectively.) You should not be misled into assuming, for example, that the use of *sh* means that *s* exists as a consonant that does not need a vowel.

- The sounds in the *-ya*, *-yu*, *-yo* columns are used mostly in words of Chinese origin, or in recent times foreign words. They are rare in native Japanese words. It would seem likely that these sounds represent an elision (contracting or combining) over time of two separate sounds *ki* (or other sounds ending in *-i*) and *a* (or *o* or *u*), using a "glide sound" equivalent to *y*. Sometimes, as for example *ja* or *sho* or *chu*, a *y* is not written in modern Romanization as it is already considered to be inherent in the sound combination. (It was written in earlier systems, as in *sya* for *sha*.)

3.2 Pronunciation

As mentioned before, pronunciation is very difficult to show in a written text, especially given the wide variation in pronunciation of English words that we might use as examples. However, we will try to give some hopefully universally understood indication of how Japanese is pronounced.

3.2.1 Vowels

There are five basic vowels in modern Japanese, corresponding (in Romanized letters) to the five English vowels "a, e, i, o, u," but in a different order. Their pronunciation is less variable than their English equivalents.

a   Similar to the first part of the vowel sound in "bite."

i   Similar to a shorter version of the vowel sound in "beat."

u   Similar to the vowel sound in "boot" but without rounding the lips.

e   Similar to the vowel sound in "bed."

o   Similar to the first part of the vowel sound in "boat" in American English.

3.2.2 Consonants and consonant + vowel combinations

These are generally similar to the English versions (both American and British) with the following exceptions.

tsu   This combination is rare in English, but is found in **tsunami**, one of the Japanese words now incorporated into English. The **ts** in this sound is similar to the **ts** of "cats."

hi   The **h** in this case is closer to a German *ch*, as in *ich*, than it is to an *h* as in "heat." That is, it is given more air friction.

fu   This is somewhere between an *h* and an *f* in English, rather like the gentle blowing out of a candle.

r   This is a flap, made by flicking the tongue against the ridge behind the upper teeth (a similar position to the English *d* or *l*). It has been likened to the *r* in the British English "very," and the *t* in the American English "water." It is not rolled. Some Japanese will pronounce the **r** more like an *l* when it starts a word (or after a nasal **-n**).

g   This is always hard, as in "get," and never soft as in "gene." Between vowels it will often become nasalized, similar to *ng* in "singer."

-n   This is a mora in its own right and is given equal length to the other moras. It varies somewhat depending on what sound follows it, the main point to note being that before **p**, **b**, or **m** it comes closer to an **m** sound. In fact, some Romanization systems actually write an **m** in such cases, as e.g. **shimbun** for **shinbun** (newspaper), though this practice is now considered a little old-fashioned and we do not follow it here.

3.3 The long and the short of it: vowel length

All the vowels can be doubled, but it is particularly common with *o* and *u*. Also, a long *o* sound can be produced not just by doubling the *o* but also by adding *u* to *o*—in fact, this is more common than a straightforward doubling.

There are a number of possible conventions for expressing a long vowel in Romanization. Some systems simply write the vowel twice, as *uu*, and in the case of long *o*, write either write *oo* or *ou* as the case may be. Other systems write *oo* even when it is technically *ou* according to the kana script, for consistency of pronunciation. Another system indicates long vowels (including *o+u*) by means of a circumflex accent (e.g. *ô*). However, the most widely used nowadays is probably the macron, a hyphen-like mark written over the letter, e.g. *ō* (though a long *i* is still usually written double rather than with a macron, for visual clarity). Unfortunately macrons are not always readily available in word-processing applications, and you may need a special font or overstrike function. Thus you may find the circumflex the more convenient.

Most Romanized dictionaries nowadays use macrons (except for double *i*). Thus, when looking up, say, *ōkii* (big), you would look up under *o+k*, whereas a dictionary using a Romanization system that doubled the vowel would require *o+o+k*. For your convenience we use the macron system in the text of this book. Please note, however, that a doubling of the vowel is preferred by some phonologists since it enables pitch differentiation to be indicated within a long vowel.

It has become acceptable to leave out the macron, or indeed any indication of vowel length, in proper nouns, especially if they are well known. Thus **Tokyo** is acceptable though technically it should actually be **Tookyoo** or **Toukyou** or **Tôkyô** or **Tōkyō**. Some people extend this license further and omit any indication regardless of word-class, but this can be dangerous unless all parties are aware of the terminology.

Note also that almost all long *e* sounds, other than in foreign words, are actually *ei*, though again some systems use only *ee* in Romanization.

You need to pay attention to vowel length not only because as a general principle you should try to get your pronunciation as accurate as possible, but also because it can get you into trouble if you don't. For example, **shufu** is a housewife but **shūfu** is an ugly hag. Other commonly cited examples of potential disaster include failing to distinguish between **shujin** meaning "husband" and **shūjin** meaning "prisoner," and similarly **komon**, a fairly old word meaning a "consultant," and **kōmon** meaning "rectum." Actually, in the latter examples, there is less room for misinterpretation since the pitch accent differs—but then again, if you don't pay attention to pitch either...!

FIGURE 3a: Oops! I didn't quite mean to say that!

3.4 Double consonants

Certain consonants—**k**, **s**, **t**, and **p**—can also be doubled. So too, for the rendition of foreign words, can their hardened forms (though **bb** is extremely rare).

As we shall see in Part Four, in kana script this is done by inserting a little (literally smaller) symbol for **tsu** in front of the symbol whose consonant is to be doubled. In such cases it is not actually pronounced as **tsu**, but indicates a little catch in the voice—equivalent to a mora in its own right—so as to give extra "preparation time" to the following consonant, effectively doubling it rather like the double *t* in "nighttime," or the double *k* in "bookkeeper." Hence it is expressed in Romanization by a simple doubling of the consonant rather than writing *tsu* in a smaller font, which could be confusing. Note that in the case of *ch-* the doubled form is written *tch-*, and similarly *sh-* becomes *ssh-*.

Like the moraic sounds with *-ya* etc., these double consonants are used particularly (but not exclusively) for words of Chinese origin and foreign words. In the case of Chinese words, it generally indicates a slight shortening of the final syllable of a two-syllable character whose reading ends in a weak sound such as *-tsu* or *-ku* or *-chi*, where this occurs before one of the consonants mentioned above. Thus *gaku* (meaning "learning") followed by *ki* ("period") is read *gakki* ("school term") rather than *gakuki*.

And like the proper pronunciation of the long vowel, the little catch in the voice is important, for if omitted or incorrectly inserted it can catch you in a different sense, i.e. catch you out, for you risk producing an entirely different word. For instance, using the example above, *gakki* means "school term," whereas *gaki* is a fairly insulting word meaning "brat." As an example using indigenous words, *kite* means "coming" but *kitte* means "cutting"!

3.5 New sounds
Largely through the increasing introduction of foreign words, in recent times especially there has been an attempt to achieve more accurate pronunciation and spelling of these words, a move that has led (as we shall see in Part Four), to additions to the katakana script (the kana system used for writing foreign words).

For example, in the past *v* used to be written with the kana symbol for *b-*, so when Romanized, "Venice" came out as **Benisu**. However, there is now a way of expressing *v* in katakana, especially when it starts a word, so it is possible to write **Venisu** in Romanization. Some Japanese will also pronounce this as *v*, though many will still use a *b* sound and indeed prefer to write it as *b-*. In fact, some words with *b* instead of *v* have become so fixed in the language that they will very probably never change, *debiru* for "devil" being one such example. Unfortunately, though many Japanese can say *l*, there is still no way of writing this in kana and hence Romanization, so "(cigarette-)lighter" is still expressed as ***raitā***, which can also mean "writer." Such further changes may well come about in the future, though the degree of fixedness of established words probably means it will apply mostly to newer terminology.

FIGURE 3b: I wonder...

At the present, we can list the following 18 "new sounds," as in Table 3c. Please note we have listed the consonants in English order, and only put in new sounds (e.g. we do not include the already existing ***cha*** etc. in the ***c*** row). We will show you how to write these new sounds in katakana in Part Four. Since some Romanized dictionaries have not caught up with all these sounds yet, especially ***v*** and ***w***, you may have to look them up as indicated by the kana in Part Four (e.g. ***wēvu*** for "wave" might be listed as ***uēbu***). In recognition of this, we will still give certain older forms in some words in this book.

TABLE 3c: New sounds

	A	I	U	E	O
CH-				che	
D-		di	du		
F-	fa	fi		fe	fo
J-				je	
SH-				she	
T-		ti	tu		
V-	va	vi	vu	ve	vo
W-		wi		we	wo

3.6 Pitch accents

Consider, for example, the different stress in many English words such as "record" or "object." If used as a noun, the stress is on the first syllable, but if used as a verb, then it goes on the second syllable. And consider words like the verb "discount": when used to mean "give a price reduction," the stress is on the first syllable just like the noun, but when used to mean "not take something seriously" it is on the second.

Japanese does not have this troublesome feature. It does not have any stress accent in its pronunciation in terms of uneven length or force, and its syllables are pronounced in regular measured "metronome-like" fashion. In that sense it is stress-free.

Nor does it have the tones of Chinese to worry about.

It does, however, have pitch accent, whereby moras ("beats") are pitched higher or lower. This is often useful in distinguishing homophones, such as **hashi** meaning "bridge" and **hashi** meaning "chopsticks." The former is low-high (L-H), the latter high-low (H-L)—though confusingly this can differ among regional accents. Similarly the example we gave to illustrate the importance of correct vowel length (in 3.3), with **komon** meaning a "consultant" and **kōmon** meaning "rectum," would probably not have such potential for embarrassment, even if the short vowel was drawled out as a long one, if attention was paid to pitch. This is because **ko-mo-n** is H-L-L (H = high, L = low), whereas **ko-u-mo-n** is L-H-H-H. The fact that the long vowel **ō** (**ou**) in **kōmon** (**koumon**) changes pitch in the middle indicates why many phonologists prefer not to use macrons, since the macron straddles two moras and makes it impossible to indicate any pitch shift.

This book is not intended as a textbook per se but rather as a descriptive introductory survey of the language, and so we will not burden you here with the use of pitch marks. These comprise, incidentally, a following rising pitch indicated by the symbol ⌐ and a following falling pitch by the symbol ⌐. Thus the above example of **hashi** meaning "bridge," which is low-high, would be written as **ha͞shi͞**.

We strongly recommend that, when you study Japanese in earnest, you use a textbook that indicates these pitch marks, and that you start off with pronunciation guidance from a native speaker (without a strong regional accent). It may seem a little daunting at first to have this extra dimension to your studies, but you will soon adjust and benefit from it. If you ignore pitch for too long, you may find it hard to pick up later.

CHAPTER FOUR

It's Only Words?

In this chapter we introduce you to the rich range of words in Japanese. Once the building blocks of sounds have been made into words, those words in turn become building blocks for language. They are indeed the bricks, held together, as it were, by grammar. Grammar is important too, but it is fair to say that words are even more so. In a worst case scenario, you can usually communicate "pidgin-style" just by words alone, even if you botch up the grammar, but conversely it's no good having an immaculate command of grammar if you don't know enough words to apply it to.

Another reason why words matter to the learner of Japanese is that in historical times Japanese culture—not unlike a number of cultures around the world—attributed a mystical power to the utterance of words in certain circumstances. This was known as **kotodama**, literally "word-spirit." The samurai in particular were very sparse with the use of words, and when they did use them, they did not use them lightly! You should not be intimidated into thinking that you absolutely must come up with just the right word, or incorrectly conclude that the Japanese have no fun with words, but it is important that you are aware that words do have a certain power and are worthy of respect and attention, just like pronouncing them correctly.

4.1 Japanese words in English

To start off, let's make our first type group of words one that you should already be familiar with, and that is Japanese words that have already entered English to a greater or lesser degree. There are more than 100 words in this category, but we'll give you just around three-quarters of them. Even if you have never spent any time in Japan, you will probably know at least a dozen of these. Understandably, they mostly relate to well known Japanese cultural items, and are all in noun form with the exception of **banzai**.

Let's also try to put them into topic-based groups, with English equivalents, and literal meanings where appropriate. These lists are not exhaustive, and are in no particular order.

LIST 4a: Familiar Japanese words

FOOD AND DRINK

sushi	filled or topped rice-rolls
nigiri	filled rice balls ("a grasping"/"handful")
tōfu	tofu, bean-curd ("rotted bean")
sashimi	raw fish ("cut flesh")
miso	miso, soy bean paste (often as soup)
*tenpura**	tempura, lightly battered seafood or vegetables
sukiyaki	fried beef and vegetables ("fried on a spade")
rāmen	ramen, a type of noodle
soba	a type of noodle
udon	a type of noodle
satsuma	a type of orange
mikan	a type of orange
nashi	a type of apple-like pear
wasabi	a type of mustard
daikon	giant radish, usually pickled ("great root")
nori	edible dried seaweed
cha (o-cha)	tea, cf. Cockney "char"
sake	rice wine

*This is actually originally from the Portuguese *temporas*, but has become overwhelmingly associated with Japan and Japanese.

THE ARTS (INCLUDING MARTIAL)

karate	a martial art ("empty hand"/"Ryukyuan hand")
jūdō	judo, a martial art ("gentle way")
jūdōka	exponent of judo ("gentle way exponent")
jūjutsu	jujitsu, similar to judo ("gentle techniques")
kendō	kendo, a martial art ("way of the sword")
aikidō	aikido, a martial art ("way of matching spirit")
dan	a grade in martial arts
nō	noh, refined classical drama
kabuki	a popular type of drama ("song and dance skill")

bunraku	puppet theater
ikebana	flower-arranging ("bringing flowers to life")
bonsai	miniature garden(ing)/tree ("tray planting")
origami	paper-folding ("folding paper")
shamisen	three-stringed lute-like instrument
koto	harp-like instrument
haiku	17-syllable poem ("entertainer's words")
geisha	trained female entertainer ("artistic person")

CLOTHING

kimono	saree-style female garment ("wearing-thing(s)")
obi	waist-sash for kimono
geta	(wooden) sandals
yukata	casual gown
tabi	socks with separated big toe
haori	type of jacket

MATTERS MILITARY

bushi	warrior
bushidō	bushido, warrior code ("way of the warrior")
samurai	warrior ("attendant")
harakiri	self-disembowelment ("stomach-cutting")
seppuku	as harakiri, preferred term ("cutting stomach")
katana	long curved sword
kamikaze	suicide pilot ("divine wind")
shōgun	shogun, historical military ruler of Japan
ninja	samurai of strange powers ("secretive person")
banzai	long live..., hurrah for... ("10,000 years")

OTHERS

sumō	sumo-wrestling
karaoke	add-your-own-voice music ("empty orchestra")
netsuke	carved figurine
rikisha	rickshaw, man-drawn two-wheeled carriage
sakura	cherry tree or blossom (not fruit)
shintō	Shinto, Japan's native religion ("way of gods")
jinja	shrine (Shinto)
torii	stylized entrance to Shinto shrine ("bird place")
tera (o-tera)	temple (Buddhist)

manga	type of comic or cartoon ("frivolous drawings")
furo (o-furo)	Japanese-style hot bath (for soaking only)
futon	quilt, duvet or mattress
tatami	rush matting
shōji	shoji, paper sliding door or screen
koi	koi carp
tōrō	toro, stone garden-lantern ("basket with light")
tsunami	giant wave ("harbour wave")
tennō	tenno, emperor
mikado	old word for emperor
zen	Zen Buddhism
zazen	meditation (especially for Zen adherents)
yakuza	yakuza, Japan's "mafia"

So, you already have a good start in terms of vocabulary. You will appreciate that these terms are pronounced more precisely in Japanese than is sometimes the case in English (e.g. "harikari" is not correct).

4.2 English and other foreign words in Japanese

We can now move on to another group of familiar words, and that is foreign "loan words" that have been borrowed by the Japanese and now make up around 10% of Japanese vocabulary. They are known as *gairaigo* in Japanese, meaning literally "words arrived from outside." Understandably, culture-specific items such as foodstuffs figure prominently in borrowed terminology, as in almost any language, e.g. the adoption of the Italian word *spaghetti* into English—*supagetti* in Japanese. (Though curiously the Japanese refer to "spaghetti westerns" as "*makaroni uesutan*.") Technological items, usually based on the English (e.g. "engine" giving *enjin* in Japanese), are also frequently found. However, borrowed words in fact turn up in a great variety of aspects of life, even when a perfectly acceptable word already exists in Japanese. In these latter cases, use of a loan word often has a novelty value and/or suggests a certain class and status for the user.

4.2.1 The range of sources for loan words

More than 80% of loan words are from English. They have proliferated since the re-arrival of Westerners in the mid-nineteenth century and again during the postwar Occupation and beyond, but some date back to the Portuguese and Dutch in the sixteenth and seventeenth centuries.

Even in the case of these non-English words many will still be familiar and readily recognizable to English speakers: for example, **garasu** for "glass" is actually from the Dutch *glas* but to all intents and purposes can be thought of in association with the English term. There are also a small number of words from Russian (e.g. **konbināto** from *kombinat* meaning an industrial complex), Spanish (e.g. **kasutera**, meaning "sponge cake," from *castella*), and many other languages. Some words are also from modern Chinese, such as **kaban** ("briefcase") from *kapan*, whereas traditional Chinese borrowings, known as **kango** or Sino-Japanese words, are not considered loan words, and will be discussed in a later section.

Clearly, these loan words are far too many to list in full, and we can merely give you examples that show how they have been "Japanized" and, for interest's sake, where they came from. Here in List 4b we will give you some commonly encountered examples from various sources (deliberately with a focus on non-English), again in no particular order.

LIST 4b: Some common loan words from varied sources

pen	pen (English)
basu	bus or bath (English)
hoteru	hotel (English/French)
shūkuriimu	cream puff (French *choux à la crème*)
guratan	gratin (French)
piiman	capsicum (French *piment*)
ankēto	questionnaire (French *enquête*)
zubon	trousers (French *jupon*)
pan	bread (Portuguese *pão*)
tabako	tobacco, cigarettes (Portuguese *tobaco*)
mesu	scalpel (Portuguese *mes*)
biiru	beer (Dutch *bier*)
kōhii	coffee (Dutch *koffie*)
koppu	drinking glass (Dutch *kop*)
orugōru	music-box (Dutch *orgel*)
rentogen	X-ray (German *Röntgenstrahl*)
karute	clinical chart (German *Karte*)
uokka	vodka (Russian *vodka*)

The above term for "X-ray" is based ultimately on the name of its discoverer, Wilhelm Röntgen (though modern German also uses "X-strahl"). There are a number of other similar terms in Japanese based on old terms for the person who discovered or popularized an item, one of the most common being *hotchikisu* for "stapler," also once known in English as a "Hotchkiss."

We should bear in mind that sometimes foreign loan words, when coexisting with native and/or Sino-Japanese words, have particular usage patterns. For example, *raisu*, meaning "rice" is used for cooked rice in non-Japanese dishes (e.g. *karē raisu* for "curry and rice"), whereas the native term *meshi* or the Sino-Japanese term *gohan* are used for cooked rice in traditional dishes (basically, rice on a plate is *raisu*, rice in a bowl is *gohan*), and the native term *kome* refers to uncooked rice and is used in a more general sense, such as when it is a commodity. Moreover, the Sino-Japanese reading *bei-* (of the kanji for "rice") is used in most compounds relating to rice, such as *beika* meaning "the price of rice."

Do not worry too much about these finer points of what term to use and when. You will get used to them over time, and certainly in the beginning stages of communicating in Japanese, your Japanese listeners will pick up what you mean whichever term you use and will also show considerable tolerance.

4.2.2 Creative adaptation of loan words

The Japanese in earlier years gained an unfair reputation as "mere imitators." It is now recognized that they bring considerable distinctiveness and indeed flair into the modification of things that they adopt and adapt, and the same applies to language.

You therefore have to be on the lookout for the occasional difference in usage and meaning between the original and the Japanized version. Sometimes this is attributable to historical reasons or a possible simple mistake. For example, the term for a steering wheel of a car is *handoru*, from the word "handle." This is a throwback to the early automobiles that were steered by a handle rather than a wheel. Similarly the word *manshon*, from the term "mansion," is applied to a large building divided into private apartments, as opposed to its Western meaning of a large individual home.

But in other examples you can see a more creative process at work. Again understandably, most loan words entered Japanese as nouns and sometimes as adjectives (in the latter case they usually take a Japanese adjectival suffix **na** when used before a noun, e.g. **hansamu na otoko** for "handsome man"). In other cases they have developed verbal and adjectival forms—again sometimes with a rather different meaning to what you might expect from the original, which may or may not have been a corresponding part of speech. We will look at different parts of speech in Part Three, but let us simply observe here that there is a verb **shimasu** meaning "to do," which is very useful in Japanese for making nouns into verbs. For example, you can combine this with the word **kanningu**—a noun meaning "cheating in an exam" derived from the adjective or noun "cunning"—and produce **kanningu shimasu**, meaning "to cheat."

Verbs can sometimes also be made of foreign words by simply adding the verbal ending **-ru**. For example, **sabo** is an abbreviated form of the noun **sabotāju** from the French/English word "sabotage" and is used particularly in the sense of an industrial "go-slow." However, it has also been made into a verb **saboru**, which can mean "to go slow" but as a verb usually means "to play truant"/"skip classes." And if some young person invites you to **makuru**, they could possibly be using the indigenous verb meaning "to roll up your sleeves/trousers," but more likely they are suggesting you go eat under the Golden Arches at **Makudonarudo**, from which name the new verb has been coined among certain trendsetters.

As another example of creative word-building, in the 1970s the English adverb "now" became a slang adjective **nau na** or **naui** meaning "trendy"—so trendy in fact, that the term has fallen from favor in the last decade or so. (And curiously, perhaps in an odd reassertion of nationalism, **nau** was briefly replaced by the equivalent Japanese adverb **ima**, with an **-i** at the end making it an adjective **imai**. This too has now largely disappeared.) And a famous example of how original parts of speech and grammatical roles can be ignored in the adaptation process is the word **abekku**. This comes from the French preposition *avec*, meaning "with," but has become a noun in Japanese with the meaning "being with someone (you're fond of)" i.e. "a date" (for which the English-derived word **dēto** also exists).

Another means of "Japanizing" is abbreviation—common to many languages, but seemingly especially so in Japanese loan words (and indeed other word-types such as *kango*). We gave you an example earlier of **difu giya** for a "differential gear" (also sometimes abbreviated in English too, to "diff gear"), but there are many more. For example, "**pāsonaru konpyūtā**" ("personal computer") has become **pasokon** (or indeed just **piishii**), **sutoraiki** (from "strike" in the sense of industrial dispute) has become **suto**, "puncture" is just **panku**, a "convenience store" is a **konbini**, and so on. Even famous people can have their names abbreviated, such as **Burapi** standing for Brad Pitt. And let's not forget the above example of eating at the Golden Arches, **makuru**.

The most creative adaptation of all, however, is the production of "Japlish," the term itself an abbreviated (by Westerners) form of "Japanese-made English" (**wasei Eigo**). In the materialistic booms of the 1960s and 70s this saw a possessiveness reflected in terms like **maihōmu** ("my home") or **maikā** ("my car"), though in time the adjective/prefix "my" soon came to symbolize "private" rather than actually specifically "my own," with the result that you could literally say "Have you bought a new 'my car'?" In more recent times the English term **shirubā**, meaning "silver," has come to be applied to the silver-haired in society, i.e. the elderly, and now features in Japlish terms such as **shirubā haujingu**, i.e. "silver housing" meaning accommodation for senior citizens. And if they drove in their younger years, they probably drove **nōkura** cars, an abbreviation of **nō kuratchi** meaning "no clutch" or automatic—a term itself now a bit elderly.

Inventive use of English also led to the classic term **sarariiman**, meaning literally "salary man" with all its connotations—a white-collar male employee at a large company on a supposedly lifetime contract and with concomitant responsibilities of long hours. Hopefully he will get a regular **bēsu appu** ("base-up," meaning pay rise). Female employees are often termed **ōeru**, usually written **OL**, and standing for **ofisu redii**, i.e. "office lady." And for that passionate office romance, constrained by time and place, you can book a private room by the hour—or by the minute, as some unkind Westerners say of busy Japanese males—in a **rabu hoteru** ("love hotel"). Terms such as these have now entered English to some extent, not universally known in the West by any means but certainly frequently used by Westerners resident in Japan.

Even the morphology (forms) of English words can be applied to Japanese terms in some cases. For example, in English the ending "-er" or "-or" can be used to indicate a person who does something particular (writer, reader etc.). In Japan fans of the popstar Namie Amuro are sometimes called "Amurers," either written as per the English or in "Japanese" as **Amurāzu**. Likewise the English abstract noun ending "-ism" has been combined with the Japanese verb **ganbaru**, meaning "to persevere," to give **ganbarizumu**, meaning "perseverance."

Advertising is notorious for its use of loan words and Japlish, which seem to be seen by marketers (and presumably the buying public in general) as adding to the exoticness and appeal of certain goods. They are sometimes written in Romaji too, or even straight "English" (of sorts). Embarrassing phraseology with unfortunate connotations, strange names (such as the well-known classics "Pocari Sweat" energy drink, or "Calpis" energy drink, or "Creap" milk powder etc.), and way-out grammar are very commonplace, but we can note here that the spirit of creative language use involving Japlish can at times be genuinely effective. One successful advert for a sports car, for example, invited readers to **supōtii futtowāku o enjoi shite**—"enjoy sporty footwork." And of course, who could overlook the Sony "Walkman," now a household word around the world!

4.3 Native words and Sino-Japanese words

We have seen that loan words occupy around 10% of the Japanese language. As mentioned in Part One, around 45% of words in Japanese can be considered native. These are known in Japanese as **wago** or **Yamato kotoba**, both terms literally meaning "Japanese words." A similar percentage is occupied by words borrowed from China—or created in Chinese style—as far back in some cases as 1,500 years ago, and these are known not as loan words but as **kango**, literally meaning "Han words." Han refers to China, technically the Han period from 206 BC to AD 220, but in practice used of China in general long afterwards.

Many kango—or more exactly their prototypes—were borrowed in the fifth to eighth centuries, especially after the adoption and adaptation of the Chinese writing system as a basis for Japanese script. Characters were usually borrowed for their meaning, but sometimes also for their sound—which could be quite varied, even of the same character, depending on which region of China it came from, and/or the point in time (more on this in Part Four). Similarly, some Chinese compound phrases were borrowed.

Inevitably, amidst all this confusion and general emulation of things Chinese, some people, especially priests, scholars and nobles, preferred to use Chinese language or heavily sinified Japanese. Among other things, Chinese terminology could convey nuances of meaning, especially with abstract nouns, that were not necessarily easily expressed in *wago*. Also, and importantly from a socio-linguistic perspective, Chinese symbolized civilization, formality, authority, status, and a high level of education. The Buddhist sutras, for example, were written in Chinese. That is, it was rather like Latin in medieval and early-modern Europe. And again like Latin in Europe, Chinese in ancient Japan was very much a male domain, partly because few women were educated. Even educated court ladies were usually constricted to native Japanese.

Over time the fashion for Chinese proper eventually gave way to Japanese, but heavily sinified Japanese still carried great weight. These authoritative connotations were one reason why the Meiji government, following the reopening of Japan to the Western world in the mid-nineteenth century, borrowed or coined many new *kango*. Examples include **shinbun** for "newspaper" (literally "newly heard"), **tetsudō** for "railway" (literally "iron road"), and **denwa** for "telephone" (literally "electric speech"). You need to be a specialist to fathom where exactly a given word was coined. **Denwa**, for example, appears to have been coined in China, whereas **keizai**, meaning "the economy" (literally "guiding principles for a proper settling of things"), seems to have been coined in Japan. The distinction is not really important, for even in the case of clearly borrowed *kango*, these relatively modern terms are still treated as "traditional" Sino-Japanese words and not *gairaigo* loan words. (Though note the later **kaban** in 4.2.1.)

It is still largely the case today that *kango* carry weightier overtones than *wago*. In formal documents and scholarly texts, for example, they can occupy as much as 75%, with the remaining 25% being *wago* with few, if any, loan words. Proportionately they generally feature more prominently in written language than spoken, being least used in very colloquial speech.

One of the reasons for this is that *kango* tend to have relatively few and often quite similar sounds, heavily using long vowels and "expanded syllables" with *-y* (e.g. **kyūryō** "salary"), with a lot of homophones or quasi-homophones, and when verbalized are more easily confused and confusing than *wago*. (Remember that words in the Chinese language proper have distinguishing tones, whereas, apart from pitch variation, *kango* in Japanese do not.) There are, for example, no fewer than twenty words pronounced **kōkō** in Kenkyusha's *New Japanese-English Dictionary*, a standard big dictionary. If you leave out the macrons and don't bother to distinguish between short and long vowels, then the number doubles to forty. In practice only a few of the twenty **kōkō** are used verbally, the main one being the word meaning "high school" (an abbreviation of **kōtō gakkō**), so the danger here is that if you verbalize another **kōkō** that is usually only written, such as the **kōkō** meaning "pit-head," you risk being misunderstood. Usually the context and the pitch will make your meaning clear, but this may not always be the case.

Getting *kango* syllables in the wrong order also seems a problem for Westerners, even when the syllables are relatively distinct. One actual example involved a young native English-speaking student some years ago who, attempting to explain in Japanese to an audience of dignitaries that she had found accommodation with a then-rare flush toilet—**suisen benjo** (**suisen** is "flush," literally "water wash"; **benjo** is "toilet," literally "convenience place")—ended up mistakenly saying **sensui benjo**, with **sensui** unfortunately having the meaning of "scuba-diving" (literally "dive water"). The inevitable audience reaction was not unlike that of the English-speaking audience of the unfortunate Japanese ambassador, whose English was pronounced very Japanese-style, when he told them, "Please sit." (Think about it. And yes, both incidents really happened.)

FIGURE 4a: A new challenge for the adventurer?

Sometimes, especially if the kanji are the same, such a "back-to-front" mistake is not necessarily serious. For example, ***giron*** (literally "debate argument") and ***rongi*** (literally "argument debate") both mean "debate" or "discussion." On the other hand, ***kaisha*** (literally "meet gathering-place") means "company" (as in "corporation") while ***shakai*** (literally "gathering-place meet"), with the same kanji reversed, means "society" (as in "sociology").

As is common with borrowings, most *kango* are nouns, though they can often be converted to verbs (by the use of ***shimasu*** meaning "to do," as seen earlier with certain loan words), or in other cases into adjectives and adverbs. We will look at these parts of speech in Part Three.

By contrast, native Japanese words, *wago* (though ironically, unlike the term ***Yamato kotoba***, the term itself is a *kango*!) have clearer, crisper syllables, more varied sound combinations, and more distinctiveness. Take for example the *kango* term **kyōjuhō**, which means "teaching method," and contrast this with the *wago* term with approximately the same meaning, **oshiekata** (***o-shi-e-ka-ta***), meaning literally "way of teaching." Which seems the more distinctive? Which seems easier to remember? Likewise the *kango* **kyokō** and the *wago* **tsukuribanashi**, which both mean "a made-up story." You might also consider **kōshokyōfushō** meaning "acrophobia/a fear of heights," a *kango* term which could be expressed more simply in *wago* by the phrase **takai tokoro ga kowai** ("to be afraid of heights").

Of course we can sometimes do the same in English, and use simple Anglo-Saxon while avoiding almost entirely the more complicated Latin and Greek-derived terminology. For example, patients will usually use very different terminology from doctors when discussing the same ailments among themselves. But we can't do it all the time, and that is also the situation in Japanese. While it is a fact that native English speakers almost always find *wago* easier to remember than *kango*, even though they are often longer words or phrases, the two threads are very strongly intertwined in the language and one cannot simply ignore the *kango*. Sometimes there is a choice, but often there is not. In the example above, **kōshokyōfushō** is a noun, **takai tokoro ga kowai** is not, and occasionally you would need to use the noun, just as in English. And even when there appears to be a close similarity, there is often a difference in nuance. In everyday conversation you would be able to use **oshiekata** as "teaching method" instead of **kyōjuhō**, but in a more formal context, such as a conference on teaching methodology or a book on pedagogy, it would be considered inappropriately informal.

And at other times, there is simply no *wago* fully equivalent to a *kango*. For example, **kangae** is a *wago* term for "thought" or "idea," and **kangaekata** can mean "way of thinking" at an individual level, but there is no *wago* for "ideology" in the philosophical sense, and here you would have to use the *kango* **shisō** (or the gairaigo **ideorogii**). This in turn gives a range of compounds, such as **shisōshi** for "intellectual history" and **shisōka** for "thinker." *Wago* too can be used to build up compounds, as seen in **tsukuribanashi** above (from the verb stem **tsukuri** meaning "make" and **banashi** from **hanashi** meaning "story"), but generally it is *kango* that provide the richer material for this kind of word building.

Table 4a below gives a few illustrations of the actual differences (or otherwise) between seemingly similar *kango* and *wago*. In all cases, even if there is no difference in actual meaning and they are interchangeable, the *kango* is more formal in practice.

TABLE 4a: *Wago* and *kango* "equivalents"

WAGO	KANGO	MEANING
tabi	*ryokō*	"journey" (*wago* now somewhat poetic/metaphoric)
tabemono	*shokumotsu*	"food" (*kango* more in the commodity sense)
meshi	*gohan*	"cooked rice, meal" (*wago* can mean food in general or livelihood)
abunai	*kiken na*	"dangerous" (*wago* has no commonly used noun form)
wakarimasu	*rikai shimasu*	"to understand" (*kango* implies logical process, *wago* can mean "empathize")
manabimasu	*benkyō shimasu*	"to study" (*wago* has sense of "learn from teacher")
kuruma	*jidōsha*	"vehicle" (*kango* less often used for private car)

Here, we can note one distinctive feature of *wago*, and that is the rich stock, compared with *kango* and English, of onomatopoeia. This is both in the sense of reproducing an actual sound (as in the English "buzzing of bees"), such as **goro-goro naru** meaning "to rumble" (of heavy wheels, thunder etc.), and interestingly, also in describing a noiseless action or scene—known technically as mimetic (mimicking) terminology. English is poorly endowed with the latter, and we have just a few obvious examples, such as "higgledy-piggledy" and "topsy-turvy." Japanese *wago*, by contrast, include literally hundreds. Common examples include **abe-kobe**, meaning "topsy-turvy"; **fuwa-fuwa**, meaning "soft(ly)" or "light(ly)" or "fluff(il)y"; **pika-pika**, meaning "glittering(ly)" or "bright(ly)," and **kyoro-kyoro** meaning "staring(ly)." They can usually be used as adverbs, adjectives, or verbs (with **shimasu**).

You will have noticed that in these mimetic terms there is often repetition of the first word (often separated by a hyphen in Romanization, though this tends to vary case by case). This can also happen in non-mimetic terminology, especially adverbs. For example, *iro-iro* means "various(ly)" (literally "color-color"), and ***tabi-tabi*** means "frequently" (literally "occasion-occasion"). The first consonant of the second word is normally hardened if there is no other hard sound in it, e.g. ***tokidoki*** meaning "sometimes" (literally "time-time"), but ***tabi-tabi*** not ***tabi-dabi***, as the *bi* is a hard sound.

Many languages have this reduplication feature or similar (often using rhyming, e.g. the English "helter-skelter"), but its frequency in Japanese *wago* leads some linguists to see it as illustration of a Polynesian strand in the native language.

In general, *kango* prevail among nouns, especially abstract nouns, while *wago* prevail among other parts of speech, such as verbs and adjectives and adverbs and prepositions. But, as mentioned earlier, this does not mean that *kango* cannot be made into verbs, adjectives or adverbs in many cases. We will look at these parts of speech in Part Three.

Basically, making the distinction between *kango* and *wago* is interesting but not always of practical help, just as is the case in English with Anglo-Saxon on the one hand and Greco-Latin on the other. In reality, it is a case of accepting the Japanese language for what it is, i.e. a mix of these elements, and then trying to emulate what the native speakers do, following their lead as to the choice of vocabulary in given situations.

It is now time for us to move on to Part Three, which deals with how words are put together into sentences.

But first, let us just recap in List 4c some of the more useful words that have occurred in this sub-chapter 4.3.

LIST 4c: Recap of useful words from 4.3

shinbun	newspaper
tetsudō	railway
denwa	telephone
keizai	economy
kyūryō	salary

kōkō	high school
gakkō	school
*benjo**	toilet
giron	debate
kaisha	company, firm
shakai	society (at large)
oshiekata	way of teaching
kangae	thought, idea
kangaekata	way of thinking

**otearai* is a more polite word

PART THREE

Words Into Sentences

We have now seen the sounds that make up Japanese, and how these sounds are put into words. In Part Three we go to the next stage and look at how words are put into sentences. That is, we look at grammar (the overall rules), syntax (the arrangement of words) and the roles of the various parts of speech. Let's approach this as much as possible through the parts of speech, as these are generally a convenient transition from words and also give a focus to what might otherwise be fairly abstract grammar. (It should however be appreciated that in some cases a given word may be classifiable in more than one category, and that categories themselves can vary according to definition.)

Chapter Five examines the basic parts of speech—nouns, pronouns, verbs (basic tenses only), adjectives, adverbs, postpositions (similar to prepositions in English), conjunctions, and particles. The term "particle" can be confusing since it can at its broadest cover a range of short words that are also classifiable as some other part of speech, such as conjunction or postposition. However, we try to limit our usage to words that generally are not directly translatable into English but merely show a grammatical role.

Chapter Six looks at more advanced grammar, including politeness levels, and ends with some common sayings.

CHAPTER FIVE

The Basic Parts of Speech

In this chapter we will consider the types of word that make up sentences and how these are modified (or not) by grammar. We will devote a section to each basic type, though some overlap is inevitable.

5.1 Nouns, pronouns and titles

Here we consider the names of things and people, including titles and family members.

5.1.1 Nouns

The words we have looked at so far have been almost entirely nouns, as they are the most basic parts of speech. We have seen how they comprise a balanced mix of native words (*wago*) and Sino-Japanese words (*kango*), plus a smaller but growing and highly convenient number of foreign loan words (*gairaigo*). We have also seen something of the distinctive nature of each of these types, such as the long vowels and expanded syllables that characterize many *kango*.

There's not very much more to learn about nouns in Japanese. Unlike many languages, and regardless of whether they are *wago* or *kango* or even *gairaigo*, they do not change form depending on whether they are subjects or objects. That is, **inu** is "dog" whether it's the subject doing the biting or the object being bitten. Moreover, though it is possible if necessary to indicate the gender of living things, nouns themselves—including nouns for living things—do not have a grammatical gender, unlike French or German. That is, there is no equivalent of *la*, *le*, *der*, *die* or *das*. Nor, to all intents and purposes, is there any metaphoric gender ascription, so that ships, whales, countries and whatever are not referred to as "she" or "her."

Nor—and unfortunately this can be a hindrance as much as a help—is there usually any distinction between singular and plural. **Inu** can be one dog or plural dogs. Of course, if they wish, the Japanese can say "three dogs" or a "number of dogs" or "several dogs," but more often than not, they don't bother, even when the context is unhelpful. This can cause some anxiety in native English speakers used to more explicit identification, and can be a veritable nightmare for translators!

There are actually a number of plural endings, such as ***-tachi*** and ***-ra***, both usually only applied to people or other living things. (You should be careful with the word ***tomodachi*** ("friend") of which ***-dachi*** is a variant of ***-tachi***. This was originally a plural term based on ***tomo*** meaning "companion," but is now also used of a friend in the singular.) However, these plural indicators are not often used, with the exception of pronouns.

Some nouns, such as ***namae*** meaning "name," can be made polite by attaching a polite prefix ***o-***, thus ***o-namae***, which effectively means "your name." You would never do this with your own name. Through a broader concern to show both respect and elegance in expression, certain everyday nouns can also be "honored" by adding the polite prefix ***o-*** or occasionally ***go-***. This is often applied to comestibles, as in some words we have already seen, ***o-cha*** "tea" and ***gohan*** "cooked rice." And as in most societies, money (***kane***) is also respected/"beautified," so that it is normal to say ***o-kane***. Women in particular use the prefix ***o-***. There is no hard and fast rule, and indeed some young women nowadays overuse the prefix, but as in all things, be guided by native speakers.

5.1.2 Pronouns

There are various types of pronoun—e.g. personal (I, you), demonstrative (this, that), interrogative (who? what?), indefinite (someone, anything), and more. We make two main divisions here, "personal" and "others," and the more common of both these groups are given in List 5a. There are more in practice, plus sundry variants.

Personal pronouns need particular attention. The Japanese use them far less often than English speakers, particularly in polite speech, and particularly with regard to the second person (you). They prefer either to let the context make it clear who is intended, or to use names. Also, there are differences in politeness level between pronouns, and differences in usage between males and females.

But one area where they do not differ is grammatical role: like nouns, they do not change form depending on whether they are subject or object.

LIST 5a: Common pronouns

PERSONAL

I/me	by males: **watashi**, or informally **boku** by females: **watashi**
you (singular)	by males: **anata**, or informally **kimi** by females: **anata**
he/him, she/her	**ano hito**
he/him	**kare***, or formally **ano otoko no hito**
she/her	**kanojo***, or formally **ano onna no hito**
we/us	by males: **watashitachi**, or informally **bokutachi**; by females: **watashitachi**

you (plural)	by males: **anatatachi** or **anatagata**,
	     or informally **kimitachi**; by females:
	     anatatachi or **anatagata**

they/them	**ano hitotachi**
they/them (male)	**karera***
they/them (female)	**kanojotachi*** or **kanojora***
who?	**dare** or formally **donata**
somebody/anyone	**dareka**
no-one/nobody	**daremo** + negative verb

*These are relatively new pronouns and not used widely by some older people.

OTHERS

this/it	*kore*
that (by you)/it	*sore*
that (over there)/it	*are*
these/them	*korera*
those (by you)/them	*sorera*
those (over there)/them	*arera*
which? (of more than two)	*dore*
which? (of two)	**dochira**, informally **dotchi**
what?	*nani*
something/anything	*nanika*
nothing	**nanimo** + negative verb

5.1.3 Titles

When speaking directly to someone, Japanese people much prefer to use that person's name (usually family name) and/or title. Thus if speaking to Mr, Mrs or Ms Tanaka, you would normally say **Tanaka-san**, **-san** being the normal polite title. Perhaps surprisingly, it is gender-neutral. (There are gender-specific titles, but they are rarely used.) Note that it can also be used of certain common nouns such as **kyaku**, meaning "guest" or "visitor" or "client," in conjunction with the polite prefix **o-**, to give **o-kyaku-san**. Similarly gender-neutral is the even more polite suffix **-sama**, which can replace **-san** including with words such as **kyaku**. There is a very informal suffix **-chan**, normally used only of children and very close friends, which is similarly gender-neutral, and there is also an informal suffix **-kun**, used only of friends and juniors, and normally of and by males only.

A person's professional position can also be used as a formal manner of address, similar to the English in something like "President Bush" but used more broadly. Thus, given that **shachō** means "company president," one could say **Yamada-shachō**. If the surname is not used, then **-san** can sometimes be added, giving **shachō-san**, but there are limits on this. For example, **-san** cannot be added to **sensei**, which means "teacher" and should be used as a title when referring to or addressing your teacher (either as a name suffix or a stand-alone term).

Never use any title of yourself. This is usually considered pretentious and bad form in most cultures, though it may be tolerated (e.g. the English "I'm Mr Smith," to which incidentally an appropriate reply is "Oh, I thought you were Mrs Smith"), but it is something the Japanese would never even think of doing (with the exception of the family—see below).

5.1.4 Family members

Though seniors will generally use a relatively plain form of language to juniors within a family or company or established group, thereby in a sense confirming their own senior status, the basic principle of not elevating yourself (or those associated with you) to people outside these contexts is central to communication in Japanese. Let us consider how it applies to the terminology used of family members. Here it is necessary to distinguish between your own humble family and others, as well as differentiating in seniority and thus status among siblings. (There is no term meaning just "brother" or "sister.") It is one of the socio-cultural factors we mentioned earlier, which can catch the unwary native English speaker accustomed to more egalitarian terminology.

We give a comparative list of close family members in List 5b.

LIST 5b: Family members

YOUR OWN FAMILY	OTHER FAMILIES	ENGLISH EQUIVALENT
ani	*o-nīsan*	elder brother
ane	*o-nēsan*	elder sister
otōto	*otōto-san*	younger brother
imōto	*imōto-san*	younger sister
chichi	*otōsan*	father
haha	*okāsan*	mother
tsuma/kanai	*okusan*	wife
shujin	*go-shujin*	husband
ko/kodomo	*okosan*	child
musuko	*musuko-san*	son
musume	*musume-san/ojōsan*	daughter
kazoku	*gokazoku*	family
ryōshin	*go-ryōshin*	parents

Note that within your own family, appropriate levels of respect need to be maintained, so when addressing (or referring within the family to) a senior such as your father you should use **otōsan**. However, when talking about your father to someone outside your family, you should use **chichi**. Within the family, seniors may use the respectful term of themselves when speaking to juniors—as indicated above, one of the few cases in Japanese where this is permitted.

When making generalizations, the "polite" forms are not normally used. Thus **kodomo** rather than **okosan** is the general word for "children."

5.2 Main particles

Before we move on to verbs, adjectives and other major parts of speech, we need to pick up on a point made above, that nouns and pronouns do not change regardless of whether they are subjects or objects. Their grammatical role is shown partly by their placement within a sentence:

remember from Part One that Japanese is an SOV (subject-object-verb) language, not an SVO (subject-verb-object) language like English. But that role is also shown by particles—short words that do not necessarily translate in themselves (at least in the case of particles proper) but act as markers of grammatical function.

The main particles are as follows in List 5c. Perhaps confusingly, as mentioned earlier some people include as "particles" short words that are also classifiable as postpositions or conjunctions—though there can be a certain overlap (e.g. see *o* in List 5c). To avoid bombarding you with an overload of small words we have not included these here, and will address them in a later chapter. Note that most particles do not have their own pitch, for this is determined by the preceding word.

LIST 5c: Main particles

wa	topic indicator, "as for" (known subject or occasionally known object—including time and place—in main clause, sometimes as "the" in English; also a contrast marker)
ga	subject indicator (new or unknown subject, as "a"/"some"; subordinate clause subject)
o	object indicator (can also be used prepositionally, as discussed later)
no	possessive indicator; noun linker
ka	question indicator
ne	tag question indicator usually requiring answer, e.g. "isn't it?"
nē	tag question usually not requiring answer, e.g. "isn't it!"
yo	emphasis indicator, sometimes close to exclamation mark
to	quotative particle, indicating thought or speech

Rather than discuss the usage of particles in the abstract, let us move promptly onto verbs, so we can show you examples in proper sentences.

5.3 The basics of verbs and particle usage

Here we introduce you to verbs, and at the same time use these to illustrate particle usage. We discuss only simple tenses, and will dedicate a later sub-chapter to showing you more complicated verbal structures.

We give below, in List 5d, the new words we'll use in 5.3, plus a few that have already occurred.

LIST 5d: Main new words in 5.3

tomodachi	friend
kyaku	guest, visitor, client
o-kyakusan	guest, visitor, client
kakimasu	write
yomimasu	to read
kimasu	to come
ē	yes
hai	yes (usually formal)
ie	no
iie	no (usually emphatic)
yoku	often, a lot
tegami	letter
hon	book
zasshi	magazine, journal
isha	doctor
iimasu	to say
bōifurendo	boyfriend
Eikoku	England, Britain
Igurisu	England
Nihon	Japan
-jin	person from a country
*-go***	language of a country
shimasu	to do
keisan	calculation
kansatsu	observation
benkyō	study
desu	to be (copula)
gakusei	student
purezento	present, gift
jisho	dictionary
(*ni*) *narimasu*	become
jibun	oneself
heya	room
imasu	to be (locative, animate)

arimasu	to be/exist (locative, inanimate)
Pari	Paris
Furansu	France
kane	money, occasionally metal
o-kane	money

*The word for "English language" is not **Eikokugo** or **Igirisugo** but **Eigo**. The word for "American English" is **Beigo**.

5.3.1 A brief note on politeness levels

Japanese verbs can be a little daunting to the native English speaker because they are key indicators of politeness level, and Japanese is a very "politeness-sensitive" language. Sometimes entirely different sets of words have to be used depending on whether you are the subject of the verb or some other person is, and again what the status of that other person is. Also, the form of the verb, particularly its ending, reflects politeness level, in what is called "register." We dedicate a section to politeness and register later in Part Three, and until then will stick with what is called the **-masu** form, which is the safest "default" register.

5.3.2 Basic tenses

In the **-masu** form, with the part-exception of the copula "to be" (which we will discuss presently), all verbs end in **-masu** in the affirmative simple present, and **-masen** in the negative. (Remember that this tense also covers an English future tense: it's sometimes called the "non-past tense.") In the past affirmative, **-masu** changes to **-mashita**, and in the past negative **-masen** takes an additional word *deshita*. We will illustrate this below in Table 5a with reference to the verb *kakimasu*, meaning "to write."

TABLE 5a: Basic tenses

affirmative present/future (write, will write)	*kakimasu*
affirmative past (wrote)	*kakimashita*
negative present/future (don't/won't write)	*kakimasen*
negative past (didn't write)	*kakimasen deshita*

We can now make simple sentences to illustrate these tenses along with particle usage.

"I don't write letters" is ***Watashi wa tegami o kakimasen.*** This can also be translated as "I won't write a letter." (Remember that nouns can be singular or plural.)

The ***o*** indicates that ***tegami*** (letter[s]) is the object, while ***wa*** indicates that "I" is the topic (which in this case happens to be the subject too).

Imagine a situation in which a difficult letter had to be written by someone in your group, and you were discussing who this might be. One of the groupmembers might say, "Who's going to write the letter?" In Japanese, because the letter would be in everyone's mind, there's no real need to express it, so someone might simply ask ***Dare ga kakimasu ka*** (literally "who's going to write [it]?"). Interrogative pronouns, referring to something unknown, by their nature take ***ga***. You can also see here how ***ka*** makes a question. Then, as the most senior in the group, you might volunteer to do the job. You might then say ***Watashi ga kakimasu***. You would use ***ga*** here rather than ***wa*** because it is necessarily "new" information since it is in reply to a question. It also gives a certain emphasis.

In fact, though ***wa*** as the topic particle is typically used with the subject of the verb, the above example shows that the topic can sometimes be a grammatical object—a case where the English "as for" might be used. That is, a fuller version of the above question might be "As for the letter, who's going to write it?" In this case, ***tegami***, despite being the object, would come at the start of the sentence and would be followed by ***wa*** (which would replace ***o***): ***Tegami wa dare ga kakimasu ka.***

The difference between ***wa*** and ***ga*** can also sometimes be likened to the difference between the definite article "the" and the indefinite "a/some" in English. For example, using ***tomodachi*** meaning "friend(s)" and ***kimasu*** meaning "come," we can make two sentences:

Tomodachi wa kimashita = My/The friend came.
Tomodachi ga kimashita = A friend came.

The former would imply that your friend was expected and duly arrived, the latter that s/he turned up rather unexpectedly.

The difference between **wa** and **ga** is one of the trickier aspects of basic Japanese for beginners—numerous theses have been written on it—but you will soon get the hang of it through exposure and practice. After all, the Japanese have!

We mentioned in List 5c that **wa** could also be a contrast marker. An example (using **keredomo** meaning "but') might be: **Tomodachi wa zasshi wa yomimasu keredomo, hon wa yomimasen** ("My friend reads magazines but doesn't read books"). Here we have **wa** used both of the topic/subject and the contrasted object in the same sentence.

We can also use one of the above examples about the letter to illustrate the emphatic particle **yo**. That is, we could add it to the sentence **Watashi ga kakimasu** to give **Watashi ga kakimasu yo**. This just gives a little more emphasis, something like "It's me who's going to write it."

(As a little diversion here, think about people learning English. How would you explain to them that it is more natural to use "me," the object form, when grammatically it is "I," the subject form, that should theoretically be used here? It's not just Japanese that has its little quirks!)

We can also use it to illustrate the tag-question particle **ne**. One of the group might say to you "You are going to write it, aren't you?" He or she would almost certainly not address you as **anata**, but would use your name and/or title. So, if you were called John, their question might be phrased **Jon-san ga kakimasu ne,** to which you might reply variously (**Ē,**) (**watashi ga**) **kakimasu** (**yo**). Or, of course, you could reply (**Ie,**) **kakimasen** (**yo**).

By contrast, the more emphatic tag question **nē** could be illustrated by a situation in which someone remarked "You write a lot, don't you!" Here "a lot" would be more naturally translated into Japanese by "often" (**yoku**), giving **Yoku kakimasu nē**.

The particle **no** basically links nouns, more often than not in a way that indicates possession or belonging. Among other things it is similar in meaning to the English "of," but is perhaps best thought of—because of the word order—as the so-called "Saxon S," as in "John's letter." That is, the possessor/creator precedes the possessed/created, so in Japanese this would be ***Jon-san no tegami***. The word for "to read" is ***yomimasu***, and thus the sentence "I didn't read John's letter" would be (***Watashi wa***) ***Jon-san no tegami o yomimasen deshita***.

Note that ***no*** also makes pronouns into possessive pronouns or adjectives: i.e. ***watashi no*** is "mine" or "my." Thus "Did you read my letter?" is ***Watashi no tegami o yomimashita ka***, while simply "Did you read mine?" is ***Watashi no o yomimashita ka***.

The same particle can also link nouns in a case where we might in English just place them together (called apposition) or use a hyphen. The larger category comes first, such as in ***tomodachi no Jon-san*** meaning "John, (one of) my friend(s)" or "my friend John" (as opposed to ***Jon-san no tomodachi***, meaning "John's friend"). Let's consider a possibly clearer case such as "Englishman" or "Japanese language." England is **Eikoku** or more commonly **Igirisu** and the (gender-neutral) suffix ***-jin*** means "-person." **Nihon** means "Japan" and the suffix ***-go*** means "-language." Thus:

Igirisujin no Jon-san wa Nihongo no hon o yomimashita means "John, the Englishman, read a Japanese book."

Let's end this section with an even more complex sentence involving the quotative particle "to" with a direct quotation, the verb ***iimasu*** meaning "to say," a few uses of ***no***, and words from Lists 5b and 5d. See if you can work it out. (And no, it won't win you any prizes for style—it's just an illustration!)

Jon-san no imōtosan no Nihonjin no bōifurendo wa "Watashi wa nanimo kakimasen deshita" to iimashita.

It means: "The Japanese boyfriend of John's younger sister said, "I (i.e. the boyfriend) didn't write anything.""

Indirect quotations involve a change of verb register, so we will postpone this for a while.

You should note that there is a range of *kango* nouns that can be made into verbs with the addition of the verb **shimasu** meaning "to do." They are almost always abstract words, often equivalent to something like a noun ending in "-ation" in English. For example, the noun "calculation" is **keisan**, and **keisan shimasu** means "to calculate," while **kansatsu** means "observation" and **dareka o kansatsu shimasu** is "to observe someone." Some abstract nouns do not end in "-ation," as the earlier mentioned (in Table 4a) "study," **benkyō**. You can either say **Nihongo o benkyō shimasu**, for "I will study Japanese," or **Nihongo no benkyō o shimasu**, which translates more as "I will do a study of Japanese." We will not give you a list of these, as they number in the thousands, but be aware of their existence. They are useful vocabulary builders.

5.3.3 "To be"
The most commonly used verb in any language—and one that is often irregular—is the verb "to be." There are two types of this verb. One, called the copula (meaning "linking"), is used to say that someone or something is or isn't something else, such as "Mike is a student." The other, the locative, is used to say someone or something exists in a location, e.g. "Sarah is in her room." In English we use the same verb; in Japanese, along with many other languages, separate verbs are involved. Moreover, in the case of the locative, different verbs are used depending on whether the subject is animate or inanimate.

The formal copula is a two-word verb, comprising **de** and **arimasu**, with a regular conjugation **de arimasu**, **de arimashita**, **de (wa) arimasen**, and **de (wa) arimasen deshita**. However, the affirmatives are normally contracted to the forms given in Table 5b.

TABLE 5b: Basic tenses of copula "to be"

affirmative present	*desu*
affirmative past	*deshita*
negative present	*de wa arimasen/ja arimasen**
negative past	*de wa arimasen deshita/ja arimasen deshita**

*Some speakers make the *ja* into *jā*. *De wa* is politer than *ja*.

Thus "Mike is a student (=*gakusei*)" is ***Maiku-san wa gakusei desu***. "Mike is not a teacher (=*sensei*)" is ***Maiku-san wa sensei de wa arimasen***.

Although the locative "to be" differs depending on whether the subject is animate or inanimate, this is not the case with the copula. As an example using inanimates, "My present (=*purezento*) was a Japanese dictionary (=*jisho*)" is ***Watashi no purezento wa Nihongo no jisho deshita***.

Note that the copula is not used to indicate a future tense. Instead, usually a verb such as "to become" (here=*ni narimasu*) is used. So, "My son will be(come) a doctor" is ***Musuko wa isha ni narimasu***.

Let us now consider the locatives. To say "Sarah is in her room (=*heya*)" we need to give you a "sneak preview" of a particle/postposition, and that is the word ***ni*** meaning (among other things) "in" or "at," and it follows the location. Thus "in the room" is ***heya ni***. The locative verb "to be" for animate subjects is a regular verb ***imasu***, so the sentence is ***Sera-san wa (jibun no) heya ni imasu***. To say "The dog (=*inu*) wasn't in the room" would be ***Inu wa heya ni imasen deshita***.

Inanimate subjects take the verb ***arimasu***—the same as the second half of the copula. Thus "Paris is in France" is ***Pari wa Furansu ni arimasu***, and "It wasn't in the dictionary" is ***Jisho ni arimasen deshita***.

Both ***imasu*** and ***arimasu*** can also be used in the sense of existing in someone's possession or sphere of existence, similar to the English "to have." Thus "They have no children" is ***Ano hitotachi (ni) wa kodomo ga imasen***, and "I have no money" is ***Watashi (ni) wa (o-)kane ga arimasen***. The postposition ***ni*** is optional in such cases.

The locative is often used with postpositions, so we will discuss these next.

5.4 Postpositions and Conjunctions
The use of postpositions and conjunctions will help expand your range of expressions and knowledge of structures considerably.

But first, List 5e introduces some new general vocabulary for 5.4.

LIST 5e: New general words for 5.4

Honshū	Honshu (Japan's main island)
hako	box
tachimasu	to stand
suwarimasu	to sit
sumimasu	to live (reside)
terebi	television
fude	writing-brush
isu	chair
modoshimasu	to vomit, give back
ikimasu	to go
eigakan	cinema
eiga	film, movie
michi	street, way
arukimasu	to walk
Amerika	America
kaerimasu	to return (home etc.) (v.i.)
yūbinkyoku	post office
keisatsusho	police station
sumimasen	excuse me, sorry
tsukue	desk
kami	paper
nado	etcetera
ashita	tomorrow
kyō	today
shinshi	gentleman
owarimasu	to finish (v.i. and v.t.)

5.4.1 Postpositions

We introduced previously the postposition *ni* meaning *in* or "at," as e.g. *Hiroshima wa Honshū ni arimasu* ("Hiroshima is in Honshu").

Ni can also mean "to"/"towards" (a destination), and is also used in phrases giving more precise information about location. These are listed below in List 5f, along with common words for "here" and "there" (though technically these are adverbs), and other postpositions.

LIST 5f: Main postpositions

ni	to, at, in
e	to
kara	from
made	up to, till
o	along, through
de	in, at (where action involved), by means of
to (*issho ni*)	with, in the company of
koko/kotchi	here
soko/sotchi	there (by you)
asoko/atchi	over there
doko	where?
ue	above, on (top of)
shita	beneath, below
mae	front, before
ushiro	behind
naka	middle, inside
soto	outside
yoko	beside
migi	right
hidari	left

The words from *ue* down are often used in a structure such as *X no ue ni* (*wa*), meaning literally "in the above part of X." The topic particle *wa* may also be used if the location is the topic. Thus, if you were given a box (*hako*) and wondered what was inside it, you might ask *Hako no naka ni wa nani ga arimasu ka*. If you're lucky, a rewarding answer might be *O-kane ga arimasu yo*. (Once a topic has been established, such as being marked by *wa*, it will normally be omitted in subsequent responses or statements.)

One significant difference from English is that a different postposition/particle is required depending on whether there is action or not in a given place. More exactly, *de* is used rather than *ni* whenever action is involved—which means basically any verb except a few such as existing in a location (*arimasu/imasu*), standing (*tachimasu*) sitting (*suwarimasu*), residing (*sumimasu*), and so on. Thus *Sera-san wa heya ni imasu* is how to express "Sarah is in her room" (i.e. merely being there), but if you want to say "Sarah often watches TV in her room" you must replace *ni* with *de*: *Sera-san wa yoku heya de terebi o mimasu*. Similarly "The cat was under the chair" is *Neko wa isu no shita ni imashita*, but "The cat threw up under the chair" is *Neko wa isu no shita de modoshimashita*.

De is also used to mean "by means of," and so is sometimes called "the *de* of utility." Thus, "to write with a brush (*fude*)" is *fude de kakimasu*.

"With" in the sense of "to go with someone" is expressed by *to issho ni* or simply *to*. "To go" is *ikimasu*, and "cinema" is *eigakan*. Thus "Mary went to the cinema with a friend" is *Mearii-san wa tomodachi to (issho ni) eigakan ni ikimashita*.

Another interesting point about Japanese postpositions is the use of the object particle *o* as a postposition meaning "along" or "through." Thus "The child walked along the street" (street=*michi*, walk=*arukimasu*) is *Kodomo wa michi o arukimashita*.

When expressing the English "to" in the sense of motion, both *e* and *ni* are possible, but *ni* is normally used when there is a purpose evident or implied. Thus the general statement "My friend went to America" would normally be *Tomodachi wa Amerika e ikimashita*, though *ni* is also possible, while *ni* would be far more normal with something like *eigakan ni ikimashita*, since the purpose of watching a movie is implicit in the idea of going to a cinema (even if that's not actually what you intend to do at the cinema).

In fact, we can introduce here a purpose structure, used only with verbs of motion, that makes clear the association between *ni* and purpose. To say you are going to do something, you use the stem of the verb (that which is left when you remove *-masu*) plus *ni* plus your verb of motion. Thus our earlier example about Mary going to the cinema with a friend could be modified to *Mearii-san wa tomodachi to (issho ni) eiga o mi ni (eigakan ni) ikimashita* ("Mary went to [the cinema] to see a movie with a friend").

"From" is much simpler: "My friend returned from America" (return= *kaerimasu*) is *Tomodachi wa Amerika kara kaerimashita*, and "Mary returned from the cinema" is *Mearii-san wa eigakan kara kaeri-mashita*. Purpose or lack thereof doesn't enter into the reckoning.

Postpositions can be used with *no* in front of nouns to make them effectively adjectival, as in "a present to/from a friend," and in this case *e no* must be used, not *ni no*. Thus *tomodachi e no purezento* and *tomodachi kara no purezento*.

Though this is probably slightly confusing, it is not wrong to use the copula *desu* even of location in certain informal cases, such as when looking for something on a map and saying *Koko desu!* when you find it. Likewise, if you know there's a post office (*yūbinkyoku*) somewhere nearby, you might ask a passer-by, who tells you it is next to the police station (*keisatsusho*):

Q: *Sumimasen* ("excuse me"), *yūbinkyoku wa doko desu ka.*
A: *Keisatsusho no yoko desu.*

However, we suggest you use the locative *ni arimasu/imasu* in such cases—certainly when writing—till you become more familiar with the language. Please note too that you can't use *ni* and *desu* directly together.

5.4.2 Conjunctions
Joining things by the use of "and" or similar is simple in English but a little more difficult in Japanese.

Nouns present little problem. You simply put *to* between the nouns if the list is exclusive, and *ya* if the list is open-ended. Thus, if there are just the two items of pen and paper (*kami*) on your desk (*tsukue*), you would say *Tsukue no ue ni (wa) pen to kami ga arimasu*. If there were other things there too, which you aren't going to the trouble of itemizing for whatever reason, then you would say *Tsukue no ue ni (wa) pen ya kami (nado) ga arimasu*. *Nado* after the final item is equivalent to "etc." or "and so on," but is often left out.

A stronger way of saying "and" or "too," which can also be translated in some cases as "even," is *mo*, used directly after nouns in place of *wa/ga/o*. Thus *Tsukue no ue ni (wa) pen mo kami mo arimasu* would be equivalent to "There is both a pen and paper on the desk" (and there may or may not be other items too). You can use **mo** of just one item too, so you might add **Fude mo arimasu** to say "There's a brush too." Similarly **Tanaka-san mo kimashita** means "Tanaka came too," or "Even Tanaka came."

Mo can also be used after certain other word-types, such as postpositions and certain adverbs (though not adjectives or verbs), but care and experience is necessary here. You might want to say "There is a pen here too," with the stress on "here" as opposed to elsewhere, and this would be **Koko ni mo pen ga arimasu**. (Note the position of **mo** after **ni**. It replaces **wa**.) This contrasts with **Koko ni pen mo arimasu** ("There is a pen here as well [as other items]"). Likewise the time adverb "tomorrow" (=**ashita**) could be followed by **mo**, as in **Ashita mo ikimasu yo**, meaning "I'm going again tomorrow, you know."

However, the conjunctions **to** and **ya** cannot normally be used with anything other than nouns, and this cannot be emphasized enough—it is a major problem for native English speakers who insist on trying to use **to** to join sentences/clauses! We will discuss how to do this is in a later section, and for the interim suggest you stick with short sentences. (Again, remember that style isn't an issue at this stage.) So, if you want to say "John is an Englishman and he often goes back to England," you could just say **Jon-san wa Igirisujin desu. Igirisu e yoku kaerimasu**.

If you mean "and" in the sense of "moreover" or "furthermore," you can use the phrase **sono ue ni**. For example: "John is an Englishman. Moreover, he's a gentleman (**shinshi**)" could be **Jon-san wa Igirisujin desu. Sono ue ni, shinshi desu**.

To say "or," the particle **ka** is used between nouns, thus **Kyō ka ashita ikimasu** for "I'll go today or tomorow." **Ka** can also be used between verbs and adjectives, as we will discuss later in 6.2.8.

Another conjunction is the term "but." This is much simpler: you simply add **keredomo** to the final verb/adjective of the clause (or the shorter form **kedo** in informal circumstances). Thus, "I've got homework (=**shukudai**), but I'm not going to do it" ("to do" is **shimasu**) would be **Shukudai ga arimasu keredomo, shimasen**. (Notice that the comma in Japanese comes after the "but," not before it.) An alternative to **kedo/keredomo** is **ga**, which should not be confused with the subject particle **ga**.

Another way of expressing "but," similar to the English "however," is to make two sentences and start the second with **de mo** or **keredomo** (or **shikashi** in formal settings). Thus, **Shukudai ga arimasu. De mo, shimasen.**

Another link word for clauses/sentences is "so" or "therefore." This is also easily expressed. You can simply add **kara** instead of **keredomo** at the end of the clause. Thus, to say "I've finished (**owarimashita**) my homework so I'll watch TV," you could say **Shukudai o owarimashita kara terebi o mimasu. Kara** here is an extended use of "from," meaning something like "following from the fact that..."

Kara tends to be rather subjective, and in the case of more objective and factual grounds for some consequent action (or inaction), such as being late because your train was delayed, you would normally use **no de** instead of **kara**. This means something like "the thing is that..., so..." It's not wrong to use this after a **-masu** form, but it normally follows a plainer form, which we will introduce later.

It is important to remember how to make "so" expressions, since in Japanese there is no formal straightforward way of saying "because." In English we might say "I'm going to watch TV because I've finished my homework," but in Japanese this would usually require the clauses to be reversed to express it as a "so" clause," i.e. "I've finished my homework so I'm going to watch TV." Having said that, in modern Japanese a form of "fragmented utterance" is being increasingly used to match the English "because," i.e. **Terebi o mimasu. Shukudai o owarimashita kara.**" Note that two sentences are still required here, unlike the English.

Let's now move on to the remaining major parts of speech, adjectives and adverbs.

5.5 Adjectives and adverbs

We introduced postpositions and conjunctions before adjectives and adverbs because of their structural importance. Adjectives and adverbs give flesh to those structures, descriptively enriching the finished language product.

First, in List 5g, we introduce general vocabulary used in illustrative sentences in this sub-chapter.

LIST 5g: New general words for 5.5

hito	person, people
hitobito	people
heiwa	peace
heiwa na	peaceful
kuni	country
shinshiteki na	gentlemanly
takai	high, tall, expensive
utsukushii	beautiful
furui	old (not of people)
omoshiroi	interesting, amusing
kirei na	pretty, neat
benri na	convenient
yama	mountain, tall hill
(Fuji)-*san*	Mount-(Fuji)
yasui	cheap
sukāto	skirt
ii/yoi	good, okay
ōkii/ōki na	big
chiisai/chiisa na	small, little
dekimasu	to be possible, able to do
banana	banana
suki na	personally liked, agreeable
iya na	unpleasant, disagreeable
samui	cold (of weather)
tsumetai	cold (to touch)
atsui	hot (of weather and touch)
chairo	brown
kirai na	personally disliked
ōi	many
sukunai	few
onaji	same

mono	thing (usually tangible)
muzukashii	difficult
yasashii	easy, simple
hayai	fast, early
hashirimasu	to run
yoku	often, well
umai	tasty, skillful
umaku	well
dame na	bad, hopeless
orenji	orange
tabemasu	to eat
shōko	proof

5.5.1 Adjectives

You have already learned how to make certain adjectives using *no*, namely the possessive (e.g. *watashi no* "my") as well as "appositional" ones such as "Japanese" (*Nihon no*, or *Nihonjin no* or *Nihongo no* depending on exact meaning).

We can quickly introduce another set of related adjectives, the demonstratives. In the sentence "This is a pen" (*Kore wa pen desu*, a famous sentence in Japan as it features prominently in many English textbooks), the word "this" is a stand-alone, i.e. a (demonstrative) pronoun, whereas in "This pen is mine" the same word "this" becomes an adjective. And you have in fact already encountered another demonstrative adjective in pronoun List 5a, *ano* in *ano hito* ("he/she"), which literally means "that person." A list of demonstrative adjectives follows:

LIST 5h: Demonstrative adjectives

kono	this
sono	that (by you)
ano	that (over there)
dono	which?
konna	this sort of
sonna	that sort of, such
anna	that sort of
donna	what sort of?

Note the "qualitative" range of adjectives that end in **na**, which have a slightly different origin and different meanings from the **-no** ones. **Dono hito** means simply "which person?" whereas **donna hito** is a qualitative term meaning "what sort of person?'

There are two main adjectival types in Japanese, and **-na** is in fact one of them. It is derived from an old form of a copula and thus has strong associations with the linking of nouns. In practice, this means it is almost always used with *kango* (or *gairaigo*) rather than *wago*. For example, **heiwa** is a *kango* noun meaning "peace" and **heiwa na** (in front of a noun) the adjectival form meaning "peaceful." Thus "Japan is a peaceful country (**kuni**)" would be **Nihon wa heiwa na kuni desu**.

Because **na** adjectives are themselves very noun-like, when used after a noun they require the copula **desu**. Thus "This country is peaceful" is **Kono kuni wa heiwa desu**. That is, the adjective as such virtually disappears and we are effectively left with a structure linking the two noun concepts of "country" and "peace."

Sometimes a Chinese-derived adjectival suffix **-teki** is used between the *kango* noun and the **na**. We used the *kango* **shinshi** earlier, meaning "gentleman," and in fact we could make this into an adjective **shinshiteki na**, meaning "gentlemanly."

Unfortunately, convention means that in practice some *kango* can take **na** directly, while others will normally take **-teki na**. You will gradually get a feel for which follows which pattern, and indeed find it very useful as a means of enriching your vocabulary, just as in English we can add adjectival suffixes such as "-ish" or "-like" to nouns.

Some *kango* can indeed follow both patterns, with a fine nuance in the meaning between the two forms. For example, **heiwa na** means "peaceful" as a general state, whereas **heiwateki na** means more like "a peaceful manner in a specific context," such as "a peaceful/amicable resolution to a dispute." Don't worry about such finer points at this stage. It is not a major crime in English, for example, to make no clear distinction between "barbarous" and "barbaric."

The second major type of adjective—often called a "true adjective" as opposed to the nominal **na** type—is the **-i** adjective, which is associated with *wago*. The letter preceding the final *-i* can be any vowel except *e*, e.g. *takai* (tall, high, expensive), *utsukushii* (beautiful), *furui* (old), and *omoshiroi* (interesting). Adjectives ending in *-ei* or any consonant plus *i* are actually *na* types (e.g. *kirei na* meaning "pretty" or "neat," *benri na* meaning "convenient").

The *-i* adjectives are used without change in front of a noun (in the affirmative present at least): thus "Mount Fuji is a tall mountain" is *Fuji-san wa takai yama desu* (*yama* means "mountain"). When the adjective comes after the noun, as in "That mountain is tall," then like a *na* adjective it simply takes *desu*. Thus *Ano yama wa takai desu*.

However, Japanese adjectives inflect (change ending) like the conjugation of verbs. This is not a problem with *na* adjectives, which, like English adjectives, simply use the appropriate conjugated form of the copula (*desu*). Thus "it is convenient" is *benri desu*, "it isn't convenient" is *benri ja arimasen*, "it was convenient" is *benri deshita*, and "it wasn't convenient" is *benri ja arimasen deshita*. But the *-i* adjectives "conjugate" in themselves: that is, they incorporate the function of the copula within themselves so that *takai* more exactly means "is tall" rather than merely "tall." (And so it follows, as we shall see in a later chapter, that *takai yama* is also able to be interpreted as "a mountain which is tall," i.e. with *takai* being in itself a subordinate pre-noun clause.)

Those who are wide awake may be wondering why, if *-i* adjectives function as a copula in themselves, they need to be followed by *desu* in a sentence like *Ano yama wa takai desu*. Full marks for alertness. The answer is that grammatically *desu* is not needed: its role is rather one of indicator of register, in that it shows the level of politeness. We will discuss this further in a following sub-chapter, in which we will also discuss subordinate clauses.

For the moment, you should learn the following forms (illustrated with *takai*):

TABLE 5c: Tenses of *-i* adjectives

affirmative present	*takai desu*
affirmative past	*takakatta desu*
negative present	*takaku arimasen* (formal) or *takaku nai desu*
negative past	*takaku arimasen deshita* or *takaku nakatta desu*

Thus, using *takai* this time in its meaning of "expensive," and new words *yasui* ("cheap") and *sukāto* ("skirt"), we might make the following brief exchange (for which you shouldn't need a translation):

Q: *Sono sukāto wa kirei desu nē. Takakatta desu ka.*
A: *Ie, takaku arimasen deshita. Yasukatta desu yo.*

Be careful of the very common adjective *ii*, meaning "good" or "okay." (*Ii desu yo* is a very common expression denoting approval.) In anything other than the affirmative present it uses a variant form *yoi* (not commonly used itself in the affirmative present), giving **yoku arimasen**, **yokatta desu**, and **yoku arimasen deshita**.

Another thing to look out is that half a dozen or so *wago* adjectives can have an alternative **na** form instead of a final *-i*. The two most common are **ōkii/ōki na** meaning "big," and the opposite **chiisai/chiisa na** meaning "small." Which form to use when is largely a matter of personal taste, not grammar, but if in doubt, use the *-i* form.

On the matter of different modes of language usage from English, we should also point out that Japanese sometimes uses adjectival expressions where English uses verbal ones, such as liking and disliking. In English we say "I like bananas." If you look up a good Japanese dictionary you will find a verb **sukimasu** meaning "to like," but it is hardly ever used. Instead, the adjective **suki na** is used, to give (**Watashi wa**) **banana ga suki desu**. It is almost impossible to translate this sort of adjective into English in one word: it basically means "likable to one personally." (It is sometimes translated as "favorite," but it is not that strong, and doesn't necessarily imply that you prefer bananas over other fruit.)

You will find as well that some adjectives are vaguer or more precise than English. For example, *samui* is "cold" in the sense of ambient temperature, whereas the word for "cold to the touch" is *tsumetai*. The opposite, *atsui* meaning "hot," is the same word in both cases but has different kanji depending on whether it's hot of the weather or hot to the touch!

Some adjectives are also considered subjective, and have limited use when it comes to third parties. We will touch upon this later.

To round off this section on adjectives, we point out that you will also occasionally find other forms of adjectives, such as *-teki* used without a following *na* (in certain formal expressions), or with a *no* (again formal, and old-fashioned). Past participles of verbs, as in "a fallen tree," can also be used adjectively, as in English (we discuss these presently). You will also find *no* used with a range of nouns, such as *iro* meaning "color": *cha-iro* is the noun form of "brown" (literally "tea-color"), while *cha-iro no* is the adjectival form (e.g. *cha-iro no sukāto*). In some cases, these forms are in the process of change, so that for example *cha-iro no* is sometimes made into an *-i* adjective *cha-iroi*.

And of course, as with everything, there are traps that have been set up specifically to catch you. One of these is a number of adjectives that end in *-ai* but are actually *na* adjectives, such as *kirai na* meaning "personally disliked" (opposite to *suki na*). Another is the pair of adjectives *ōi* (many) and *sukunai* ("few"), which can hardly ever be used in front of nouns. And yet another is the adjective *onaji* (meaning "same"), which ought to be a *na* adjective, but drops *na* in front of a noun, thus *onaji mono* for "the same thing" (*mono* means "a [usually tangible] thing"). We'll let you discover other traps for yourself—it's the best way of learning!

But we will end this section with a tip to make up for that. When you build up your vocabulary, try to learn things in pairs of opposites. This is especially useful for adjectives. Then, if you forget one of them, just use the negative of the opposite. You may lose some nuance, but it will do the job most times. For example, the opposite of *muzukashii* ("difficult") is *yasashii* ("easy/simple"). If you're trying to say something is easy but can't remember the word, but through Murphy's Law you can remember the opposite, then just say *Muzukashiku arimasen*.

5.5.2 Adverbs

Whereas adjectives modify nouns, adverbs modify other parts of speech, particularly verbs. They include a range of types, one of the most common being made from adjectives. In English we typically do this by adding "-ly," and in Japanese it is not much more difficult: *-i* adjectives have the final *-i* changed to a *-ku*, and *na* adjectives have the *na* replaced with *ni*.

Thus *hayai*, meaning "fast," becomes *hayaku*, giving for example *hayaku hashirimasu* ("to run quickly"). (Note that, written with a different kanji, *hayai/hayaku* can mean "early," so in spoken language context will make it clear which is intended.) Similarly, *kirei ni* means "prettily" or "neatly," as in *kirei ni kakimasu* ("to write neatly").

A number of adjective-derived adverbs take on particular meanings. One is *yoku*, from the adjective *ii/yoi* meaning "good." The adverbial form means in some cases "well" (e.g. *Yoku dekimashita nē* meaning "You did it very well") and in others "often" (e.g. *Yoku ikimasu* meaning "[I] often go [there]"). Another is *umaku*, from the adjective *umai* meaning either "tasty" or "skillful." It is used in the common expression *Umaku ikimashita* meaning "Things went well" (as opposed to *yoku ikimashita*, which cannot be used in this sense and means instead—as shown above—"went often").

One use of adjective-derived adverbs is with the verb *narimasu*, meaning "to become." When used with an adjective, it uses the adverbial form of the adjective, which it follows. Thus "It became/got hot" is *Atsuku narimashita*. A useful *na* adjective to use as an illustration here is *dame na*, meaning "no good" or "hopeless": thus *Dame ni narimashita* means "It became hopeless" or "It didn't work out."

There are also adverbs corresponding to the demonstrative adjectives given in List 5h, and we give these in List 5i:

LIST 5i: Demonstrative adverbs

kō	like this, thus
sō	like that, thus, to that extent
ā	like that (rarely used)
dō	how, in what way?
konna ni	like this, to this extent
sonna ni	like that, to that extent
anna ni	to that extent (rarely used)
donna ni	to what extent, just how much?

Of these above words, *sō*, *dō* and *sonna ni* are used very frequently and are worth looking at a bit more closely.

The first, *sō*, occurs in a very common Japanese question *Sō desu ka*, meaning literally "Is that so?" but in practice closer to "Oh, really?" (The common reply, of course, is *Ē, sō desu*.)

Dō occurs in expressions such as *Dō shimashita ka*, meaning "What did you do?" or sometimes in the sense of "What happened to you?" It also occurs in the common question *Dōshite (desu ka)*, meaning "Why?"or "How?" or "How come?" (*Naze* has the same meaning of "Why?")

Sonna ni can be used literally, such as *Sonna ni muzukashii desu ka*, which can be equivalent to "Is it really as difficult as you describe? (i.e. 'to the extent you describe')." It can also be used, especially in negatives, in a more general sense, such as "(not) all that much": e.g. *Sāfin wa sonna ni muzukashiku arimasen*, meaning "Surfing isn't all that (i.e. not very) difficult." (In the latter case, *sō* could also be used.)

There are still other types of adverbs, such as of time and place and quantity, and usually unrelated to adjectives. You've encountered some of these already, such as *koko* ("here") and *ashita* ("tomorrow"). For your reference we give some of the commoner ones below in List 5j. See also 5.6 for more on time.

LIST 5j: Some common adverbs

taihen	very
kanari	quite, considerably
sukoshi	a little, somewhat
sukoshimo + neg.	not the least
takusan	a lot (not of time)
zenzen + neg.	not at all
zenbu	all of something
mattaku	completely
totemo	very
hijō ni	extremely
amari (ni)	too ..., too much
wari ni	relatively
dandan	gradually

As some usage illustrations:

"It's quite hot today, isn't it!"	*Kyō wa kanari atsui desu nē.*
"Jill ate lots of oranges."	*Jiru-san wa orenji o takusan tabe-mashita.*
"There's no proof whatsoever."	*Shōko wa zenzen arimasen.*
"It's not at all interesting."	*Sukoshimo omoshiroku arimasen.*
"It's completely hopeless."	*Mattaku dame desu.*

Finally, we should also draw attention again to one of the relatively distinctive features of Japanese, and that is the duplication of sounds (often but not always onomatopoeic or mimetic) that occurs particularly in adverbs. We gave some examples in 4.3, such as **tokidoki** ("occasionally"), and will not burden you further, but will just alert you to the fact that you will encounter these quite frequently. **Dandan** (literally "step-step") in the above list is just one case in point.

5.6 Numbers, dates, and times
We look now at numbers and time-related words. The two are intertwined, as many time-related words use numbers. So, we will start counting first.

5.6.1 Numbers
There are two sets of numbers in Japanese, one basically *kango*, the other *wago*, though the latter only goes 1–10. They are set out below in List 5k, which also shows you how higher numbers are built up.

LIST 5k: Counting systems

	KANGO	*WAGO*
0	*rei*	- (note *gairaigo* **zero**)
1	*ichi*	*hitotsu*
2	*ni*	*futatsu*
3	*san*	*mittsu*
4	*shi**	*yotsu*
5	*go*	*itsutsu*
6	*roku*	*muttsu*
7	*shichi**	*nanatsu*
8	*hachi*	*yattsu*
9	*kyū* or *ku*	*kokonotsu*

10	*jū*	*tō*
11	*jūichi*	-
20	*nijū*	-
21	*nijūichi*	-
100	*hyaku*	-
250	*nihyakugojū*	-
1,000	*sen* or *issen*	-
10,000**	*ichiman*	-
1,000,000**	*hyakuman*	-
how many?	*nan-*	*ikutsu*

*Shi and *shichi* are often replaced for clarity by the *wago* stems **yo(n)** and **nana** respectively, thus e.g. *jūyon* for 14 and *nanajū* for 70.
**One key point to note is that Japanese treats 10,000 as a unit in its own right, thus expressing "one million" as "one hundred ten thousands."

So, when do you use which? The answer involves another feature of Japanese, which is that certain types of objects are counted with particular suffixes. In the great majority of cases these are used with the *kango* system. There are dozens of counters, and we list some of the main ones below in List 5l:

LIST 5l: Counting suffixes

-bai	number of times (-fold)
-do	times (occasions) or degrees
-hai	cupfuls or containers-full
-hiki	(small) animals or fish
-hon	long, thin, and usually cylindrical objects
-kai	times (occasions)
-ko	general objects, usually small
-mai	thin flat objects
-nin	persons
-sai	years of age (people only)
-satsu	books

Here too **yo(n)** and **nana** are often used optionally instead of **shi** and **shichi**. Also, in the case of **-nin**, the *wago* words **hitori** and **futari** are normally used instead of **ichinin** and **ninin** (but not in higher numbers, e.g. *jūichinin*). ***Hitori de*** is the term to use for "alone, by oneself," while *futari de* means "in a twosome."

Note too that certain combinations produce slightly modified forms, such as *h* changing to *p* or *b* after -*n* (e.g. ***sanbon*** for "three pencils"), and in some cases the following consonant doubling after a shortened form of *ichi* (e.g. *issatsu* for "one book") or *roku* (e.g. *roppai* for "six cupfuls") or *hachi* (*happai*) or *jū* (e.g. *juppiki* for "ten animals"). Unfortunately, space prevents us from setting out a detailed table listing each one of these, but you will soon pick up a feel for what is right.

The *kango* system is also used for dates and times of the clock (as we shall see presently), and for measurements (e.g. ***sansenchi*** for "three centimeters").

The *wago* system is basically a default system for counting any item that doesn't have a category-specific suffix, other than perhaps -*ko* (in fact, it is possible to treat the -*tsu* ending as a counter in itself), such as "apples" (*ringo*). Thus "I bought three apples" is ***Ringo o mittsu kaimashita*** (***Ringo o sanko kaimashita*** is also possible). Notice the position of the numbers in these sentences. Beyond ten, within the *wago* system, just the number alone is used, thus ***Ringo o jūni kaimashita*** as opposed to ***Pen o jūnihon kaimashita***.

The numbers "one," "two," "three" etc. are cardinals. To make ordinals ("first," "second," "third"), you simply add a suffix -*me* to the *wago* number, or to the *kango* plus counting-suffix. Thus ***hitotsume*** (as a noun) is "the first one." If used adjectivally with a following noun, it takes a *no*: thus ***goninme no gakusei*** for "the fifth student."

5.6.2 Dates and times
We begin this section with a list of some more useful time words, mostly used adverbially.

LIST 5m: Some time words

ima	now
kinō	yesterday
konshū	this week
senshū	last week

raishū	next week
kongetsu	this month
sengetsu	last month
raigetsu	next month
kotoshi	this year
kyonen	last year
rainen	next year

Dates and times are relatively easy once you've mastered the *kango* counting system, for in most cases you simply add to it the appropriate suffix for the time-point or period.

Let's start off with hours and minutes. Hours take a suffix *-ji*, and minutes *fun*. So, if asked *Ima nanji desu ka* ("What time is it now?"), and it was "two fifty," you would reply *Niji gojuppun desu*. (You can also say *sanji juppun mae*, for "ten to three," but we suggest it's easier to use the digital form.) Apart from *desu*, points in time take *ni*. Thus "I came at one o'clock" is (*Watashi wa*) *ichiji ni kimashita*.

Duration of hours requires *jikan*, thus *Nijikan machimashita* ("I waited two hours"). *Funkan* is possible for duration of minutes, but *fun* by itself can also suffice. Thus *Gofun(kan) machimashita*. Note that the word *jikan* is also used as a general word meaning (short-term) "time," as in *Jikan ga arimasen* ("I don't have time").

Days of the month are a bit trickier. They can be counted with *-nichi*, but days up to and including the tenth are more normally counted with *-ka* with the *wago* system, and within that there are one or two exceptions. The days for 1st–10th are: *tsuitachi, futsuka, mikka, yokka, itsuka, muika, nanoka, yōka, kokonoka, tōka*; the 14th and 24th are *juyokka* and *nijuyokka* respectively while the 20th is *hatsuka*. Duration can be formed by adding *-kan* to either system (except to *tsuitachi*, "one day" being just *ichinichi*), thus *mikkakan* for "three days."

Days of the week all end in *-yōbi*, as List 5n shows:

LIST 5n: Days of the week

nichiyōbi ("sun day")   Sunday
getsuyōbi ("moon day")   Monday
kayōbi ("fire day"/"Mars day")   Tuesday
suiyōbi ("water day"/"Mercury day")   Wednesday
mokuyōbi ("wood day"/"Jupiter day")   Thursday
kin'yōbi* ("gold/metal day"/"Venus day") Friday
doyōbi ("earth/soil day"/"Saturn day")   Saturday

*Note in passing how an apostrophe is used to separate *kin* from *yō*, to distinguish from a possible interpretation as *ki* plus *nyō*. You will find this in a number of other Romanized words, though not all writers of romaji use this convention.

Weeks of duration are **-shūkan**, thus **Sanshūkan hatarakimashita** ("worked") for "I worked for three weeks."

As set out in the list below, months of the calendar take **-gatsu** on the *kango* numbers, thus **jūnigatsu no nijūgonichi** for "December the 25th." Months of duration are a little tricky: they do not simply add **-kan**, but change the **gatsu** to **getsu** and moreover "prefix the suffix"(!) with **ka-**, to give **ikkagetsu**, **nikagetsu** etc.

LIST 5o: Calendar months

ichigatsu   January
nigatsu   February
sangatsu   March
shigatsu   April
gogatsu   May
rokugatsu   June
shichigatsu   July
hachigatsu   August
kugatsu   September
jūgatsu   October
jūichigatsu   November
jūnigatsu   December

Years take **-nen** on the *kango* number, and in the case of duration may as an option also add **-kan**. Japanese are all familiar with the Western system of numbering years, such as 2003 (**nisen sannen**), but many still prefer the Japanese system, which is based on imperial reigns. Emperor Akihito acceded in 1989, which became the first year of the **Heisei** period (**Heisei** literally means "Complete Peace"). Thus 2003 is **Heisei** 15 (**Heisei jūgonen**). Be careful of the maths here, for it fools a lot of Westerners. 1989 is Year One, so 1990 is **Heisei** 2 and so on, meaning that your base-figure for adding years must be 1988 and not 1989. The preceding **Shōwa** period ("Illustrious Harmony") of Emperor Hirohito's reign started in 1926 so we must count from 1925. Thus 1989, the year of his death, was **Shōwa** 64 as well as **Heisei** 1. (The first year of a reign has a special term **gannen**, meaning "start-year," thus **Heisei gannen**.)

* * * * * *

We have now covered the basics of Japanese grammar and sentence formation. If you are keen to expand your knowledge of grammar and general usage, you will find Chapter Six useful. Even if you are not keen, you should in any event read 6.1, on plain forms and politeness.

CHAPTER SIX

More Advanced Usage

Here we extend your acquaintance with Japanese. First we look at plain forms and general issues of politeness, then somewhat more advanced grammar, then further aspects of politeness known as "respect language," and then end with some sayings (greetings, proverbs and tongue-twisters).

6.1 Politeness and plain forms

We consider here ways in which levels of politeness are determined. Some of these may be considered more or less optional, but others are important to certain fairly basic structures in Japanese.

6.1.1 General principles of politeness

So far we have used the polite and widely used **-masu** form of verbs and the equivalent **desu/-masu** form of post-noun adjectives. Apart from particles, which are seen as unrelated to register, the words that end sentences (or main clauses) are almost always verbs or adjectives, and it is these sentence-ending verbs and adjectives, and more particularly their own endings, that largely determine the register or politeness level of a sentence. This is sometimes called a "deferential" way of showing politeness, since it shows respect to the person being addressed.

Another and less deferential form is called the plain form, and when used of sentence-final verbs and adjectives this lowers the level of politeness towards the person being addressed. We will be looking at plain forms in the next section.

Another major principle of politeness, as mentioned earlier, is humbling yourself (and those associated with you) and conversely elevating others (especially the second person, i.e. the person you are addressing). This can be done in a variety of ways, including using special sets of certain words that are considered "depreciatory," used for humbling the subject of a verb, and "honorific," for elevating the subject of a verb. The very structure of any verb can also be changed to show these levels, not just the ending.

One major way of differentiating between the humble self and the elevated other party, one that is central to various verbal concepts, is that when an action is performed that involves other persons, then that action is seen as being "offered up" or "given down"/"bestowed," depending on the subject and situation. Of course, in practice this means you (and in most cases your associates), in your lowly status, are invariably offering up to others and never giving down (with the occasional exception of animals and younger siblings!). And obviously others are always giving down to you as some sort of favor—from your perspective, that is, though from their own perspective they themselves would usually see the same action as one they were offering up to you. In a sense, it could be said that Japanese speakers often compete to achieve the lowest status (at least in terms of expression)!

Thus, to use a clear-cut illustration, whereas in English we would simply say "The teacher explained it to me" (though the more considerate amongst us might insert the adverb "kindly"), the Japanese would say "The teacher bestowed an explaining (upon me)." (We deliberately use a gerund here as that is what happens in Japanese, as you will see in a later section.) The ranking in this particular illustration is quite clear, but it can be less so when you are referring to a third party doing an action involving another third party. In such a case, you often end up effectively having to "take sides," and then humbling the party you have chosen. This is where contextual knowledge of relativity of status can be helpful.

In any language it is always important to be aware of politeness and the possibility of offence being taken by the other party. In languages such as English this is usually confined to judicious choice of vocabulary in certain situations, but in the case of Japanese it is a major socio-cultural element in everyday language to the point where it plays a significant role in sentence conceptualization. Moreover, in comparison with English there is a much stronger social obligation on women to use polite language than is the case with men (even within their own home in some cases), and also amongst men there is a similar obligation for those considered to be in a junior status.

We will return to politeness in a later section on "respect language."

6.1.2 Plain forms

At a politeness-level lower than the **-masu** form is the plain form, also known as the dictionary form (in the affirmative present) since it is the form normally used for dictionary entries. It is not actually impolite in itself, and is widely used between acquaintances and in most "neutral" forms of writing, such as novels and newspapers, but it is a register you should avoid when speaking to seniors or people you are not well acquainted with. The exception is with subordinate verbs and pre-noun adjectives, where it is normal to use the dictionary form even if the sentence-final word is in the **-masu** form. It will not affect the register in such cases.

Apart from a handful of irregulars, there are basically two types of verbs in Japanese when considering the plain form: **-ru** verbs and **-u** verbs. (The latter is often divided further into half a dozen or so categories, each treated separately, but we will try to simplify this here.)

The term **-ru** verbs actually refers only to verbs ending in **-eru** or **-iru**, though just to make life fun there are some verbs ending in **-eru** or **-iru** that are not classed as **-ru** verbs! We will mention these in a moment. First, let us take some regular examples, with whose **-masu** form we are already acquainted, **taberu** (**tabemasu**) meaning "to eat" and **miru** (**mimasu**) meaning "to see"/"to watch," and list their basic tenses in Table 6a below.

TABLE 6a: Basic tenses of plain -ru verbs

TENSE	TABERU	MIRU
affirmative present / future	*taberu*	*miru*
affirmative past	*tabeta*	*mita*
negative present	*tabenai*	*minai*
negative past	*tabenakatta*	*minakatta*

As you can see, when going into the **-masu** form, **-ru** verbs replace the final **-ru** with **-masu** (or **-mashita** etc).

-U verbs are a bit trickier than *-ru* verbs because tense changes involve a variety of forms, depending on the letter that precedes the final *-u*. However, in principle, when going into the *-masu* form, *-u* verbs replace the final *-u* with *-imasu* (or *-imashita* etc). This is easier to explain in romaji, because in the kana script, such a change entails a different kana symbol involving the preceding letter, e.g. *kaku* going to *kakimasu* requires the symbol for *ku* to be replaced with that for *ki*.

There are in effect nine main sub-categories. Examples are listed below in Table 6b.

TABLE 6b: Basic tenses of plain *-u* verbs

	AFFIRMATIVE PRESENT	AFFIRMATIVE PAST	NEGATIVE PRESENT	NEGATIVE PAST
kaku ("write")	*kaku*	*kaita*	*kakanai*	*kakanakatta*
oyogu ("swim")	*oyogu*	*oyoida*	*oyoganai*	*oyoganakatta*
kasu ("lend")	*kasu*	*kashita*	*kasanai*	*kasanakatta*
katsu ("win"*)	*katsu*	*katta*	*katanai*	*katanakatta*
shinu ("die")	*shinu*	*shinda*	*shinanai*	*shinanakatta*
kau ("buy")	*kau*	*katta*	*kawanai*	*kawanakatta*
yobu ("call")	*yobu*	*yonda*	*yobanai*	*yobanakatta*
nomu ("drink")	*nomu*	*nonda*	*nomanai*	*nomanakatta*
uru ("sell")	*uru*	*utta*	*uranai*	*uranakatta*

*Remember from Table 3a that this is really a *t* preceding the *u*, as opposed to the *s* proper as in *kasu* etc., and that the addition of *s* after the *t* is merely an expedient guide in Romanization to a more accurate pronunciation of *tu*.

Note the tenses of verbs like *uru*, which have a vowel other than *e* or *i* preceding the *ru* and are not *-ru* verbs but *-u* verbs. Confusingly, there are a handful of these verbs which do in fact have an *e* or *i*, and which have to be mentally filed away as exceptions. We will not burden you further with a list, but common examples include *kaeru* meaning "to return home" (e.g. past *kaetta* not *kaeta*, as opposed to the *-ru* verb *kaeru/kaeta* meaning "to change" [v.t.]), and *kiru* meaning "to cut" (*kitta* not *kita*), which should be distinguished from the *-ru* verb *kiru* meaning "to wear/put on" (different characters, of course, when written).

MORE ADVANCED USAGE **101**

Note also that the negative ending **-anai**, as opposed to the affirmative ending **-u**, is preceded by the glide **w** when following a vowel, thus giving **kawanai** as opposed to the harder-to-pronounce **ka-anai**.

You should further note that the verb **iku/ikimasu** ("to go") has an irregular past plain affirmative, namely **itta** not **iita**. Also the plain form of **shimasu** ("to do") is **suru** not **su**. Its other forms are **shita, shinai, shinakatta**. The verb **kimasu**, meaning "to come," goes **kuru, kita, konai,** and **konakatta**.

Because of the overlap between verbs and adjectives, adjectives too have their plain forms. We give examples below in Table 6c (**hen na** means "strange").

TABLE 6c: Basic tenses of plain adjectives

TENSE	*TAKAI*	*HEN NA*
affirmative present	*takai*	*hen na / hen da*
affirmative past	*takakatta*	*hen datta*
negative present	*takaku nai*	*hen de wa nai / hen ja nai*
negative past	*takaku nakatta*	*hen de wa nakatta / hen ja nakatta*

In the case of the **na** adjective, there is a slight change depending on whether it precedes the noun or follows it. **Hen da** is the sentence-final form, but this changes to **hen na** in front of a noun. In the case of the others where alternatives are given, **hen de wa nai** and **hen de wa nakatta** tend to be the pre-noun form, but this is merely convention and not a hard and fast rule.

In point of fact, the use of any adjectival form other than the affirmative present in front of a noun is very uncommon, since in the great majority of cases it is the final verb/adjective that determines the overall tense and whether it is affirmative or negative. Thus "It was an expensive book" would almost always be **Takai hon deshita** and not **Takakatta hon desu**, and similarly "It is not an expensive book" would be **Takai hon de wa arimasen** and not **Takaku nai hon desu**. You would only change the tense of the pre-noun adjective for particular emphasis, such as "It is a book that was once expensive." However, when occurring at the end of a sentence, then it would necessarily change: e.g. "This book wasn't expensive" would be **Kono hon wa takaku nakatta (desu)**.

The **na** adjective in the above table also largely illustrates the plain form of the copula—**da** or **de aru, datta** (occasionally **de atta), de nai** or **ja nai**, and **de nakatta** or **ja nakatta**. And similarly the **da** form is never used in front of a noun. In this case **de aru** would be required—though again such a form of expression would be unusual in the affirmative, and more commonly found in the negative, as in **Nihonjin de nai hito** ("a person who is not Japanese").

Also illustrated is most of the plain form of the slightly irregular **arimasu**, which goes **aru, atta, nai** (not **aranai), nakatta** (not **aranakatta**).

To avoid the possibility of inculcating less than appropriately polite patterns in you, we will try to avoid giving you examples of the plain form in sentence-final or even main clause-final positions. Instead, we will illustrate them in the following section in subordinate clauses, in which they are perfectly acceptable even in the politest levels.

6.1.3 Subordinate clauses

A main clause is one that can stand alone as a sentence, whereas a subordinate clause is one that cannot (at least without restructuring). For example, "That man is an American" is a single main clause forming a sentence, whereas "That man who bought the book is an American" adds the subordinate relative clause "who bought the book," giving us more information about the man. We could build this sentence up further by giving information about the book, such as "That man who bought the book which my friend wrote is an American," etc. Basically, unless used in a question, "wh-" words in English (or equivalent when replaced by "that") indicate a subordinate clause, and are known as relative pronouns.

Relative pronouns simply do not exist in Japanese. You cannot use **dare**, for example, in the above sentence as a translation of "who," for such pronouns are only ever used interrogatively (i.e. in questions). So what do you do? The answer is "nothing." You simply omit it.

Let's go step by step. The main clause-cum-sentence is *Ano otoko no hito wa Amerikajin desu*. Remember that we use the *-masu/desu* form here for our main verb. To say "who bought the book" in the subordinate clause we do two things: first we forget "who," and second we put the verb into the plain form. So *hon o kaimashita* becomes *hon o katta*, and it goes in front of the item it is qualifying. Thus *Hon o katta (ano) otoko no hito wa Amerikajin desu*. (*Ano* would normally be dropped.)

Similarly, if we wished to qualify "book" with "which my friend wrote" we would first forget the "which" and second drop the clause into the plain form, meaning *tomodachi ga kakimashita* becomes *tomodachi ga kaita*. This gives us *Tomodachi ga kaita hon o katta otoko no hito wa Amerikajin desu*.

A point to note is that the subject (nominative) of subordinate verbs is almost always followed by *ga*, with *wa* reserved for the main subject (topic), which here of course is the man. (You will occasionally find the variant *no* used instead of *ga* in subordinate clauses with no real change of meaning—we could have said *tomodachi no kaita hon*—but we suggest you stick with *ga*.)

For those who are now getting carried away with a desperate urge to add subordinate clauses everywhere, you might think how you could qualify **Amerikajin**. Perhaps he was someone whom I met yesterday. This would be *watashi ga kinō atta*, though usually the *watashi ga* would be omitted if the context made it clear that it was I who met him. This would give *Tomodachi ga kaita hon o katta otoko no hito wa watashi ga kinō atta Amerikajin desu*. But we are starting to get a little unnatural here!

On the matter of omissions, remember that in English too we often omit relative pronouns, as in "the book I bought," where we omit "which" or "that." Do not be fooled by any such omission into thinking that "I bought" is not a subordinate relative clause.

And still on omissions, in English we take liberties with the prepositions that often accompany relative pronouns, so that "the person to whom I was talking" (and how many people use "whom" nowadays?!) usually becomes "the person I was talking to." Similarly "the knife with which I cut the cake" becomes "the knife I cut the cake with." This is no problem in Japanese, because not only are relative pronouns omitted entirely, so too are any of the prepositions that might have accompanied them. Thus "the chair on which I sat" loses both "which" and "on," to give simply **suwatta isu**. This can occasionally be confusing, as technically it could be translated as "the chair which sat (down)" which obviously doesn't make much sense. However, if you said **suwatta neko**, it might be a different story—was it the cat who sat down, or was it the cat someone sat on? This shows that, compared to English, Japanese is relatively context-dependent.

Two useful items to use with plain forms and subordinate clauses are **tsumori** and another use of **no**.

Tsumori means "intention," so (**Watashi wa**) **ashita iku tsumori desu** means "I intend to go tomorrow." (This is an illustration, in fact, of a different type of subordinate clause in English, a noun clause headed by a verbal infinitive "to ...") You will find a number of words that function in a more or less similar pattern to **tsumori**, such as **wake** for "meaning" (as in **Kyō ikanai wake desu ka**: "Does this mean you're not going today?").

You will have noticed that **no** occurs in quite a number of contexts in Japanese. Another usage is as a noun (technically a "substantive") meaning "thing," "one," "case," "situation" or similar. For example, in English we might say, comparing purchases with someone, "The one I bought was really good value." Japanese uses **no** like the English "one," but in a wider range of uses, and they all follow the plain form.

For example, **katta no** can mean "the thing which someone bought" (e.g. **Katta no wa hon desu**), "the person who bought" (e.g. **Katta no wa Amerikajin desu**), "the place where something was bought" (e.g. **Katta no wa Tōkyō desu**), "the date/time when something was bought" (e.g. **Katta no wa kyō desu**), or even "the fact that something was bought" (e.g. **Katta no wa yokatta desu**—"It was good that I bought it"). In fact, this structure "past plain **no wa** X **desu**," is commonly used as an emphatic structure, such as "It was John who bought it" (**Katta no wa Jon-san desu**). Note how Japanese uses a present tense copula in this last case.

One thing to note is that a repetition of **no** to give **no no** is in fact what we might fittingly call in English a "no-no": that is, it's not permissible. Thus "my one" is not **watashi no no** but simply **watashi no**, i.e. the same as the demonstrative pronoun meaning "mine."

We should also draw your attention to the word **koto**, which is often interchangeable with the substantive **no** but only in an abstract sense, never tangible. Thus, in the above examples, we could only use **koto** in the one meaning "It was good that I bought it," giving **Katta koto wa yokatta desu**. Like **no**, it is often a useful way of making a noun from a verb, such as **taberu koto** meaning "eating." It tends to be used more in generalizations than does **no**, but there is considerable overlap.

Koto is often used after a plain past to convey the tense "I have plus past participle." Thus **Pari e itta koto ga arimasu ka** would translate as "Have you ever been to Paris?" (literally "Does there exist a case of your having gone to Paris?"). It can also be used with a plain non-past, such as, by way of answer to the above question: **Ē, yoku ikimasu yo. Berusaiyu ni iku koto mo arimasu** ("Yes, I go often. There are occasions when I go to Versailles too.")

Koto after a plain form in fact produces a number of expressions, such as "to arrange to do." This uses the verb **shimasu** ("to do"), with **ni**. **Pari ni iku koto ni shimashita** means "I arranged to go to Paris." If **shimasu** is replaced by **(ni) narimasu** ("to become"), then it refers to an arrangement that has been made, not necessarily by yourself: **Pari ni iku koto ni narimashita** means "It's been arranged that I go to Paris."

Both **koto** and **no** are often preceded by **to iu** (the plain form of **iimasu** meaning "to say/call," plus the quotative particle). This means literally "called" but in fact it acts just as a link between what might often be a long and awkward qualifier clause and the noun—not unlike the English insertion of "that." For example, "The fact (that) students don't do much homework nowadays is a problem (**mondai**)"—**Ima no gakusei ga amari shukudai o shinai to iu koto wa mondai desu**.

To iu(/**to iimasu**) is used more literally with the plain form to report indirect speech. Thus "Ken said he would go tomorrow" is **Ken-san wa ashita iku to iimashita**. Note also in passing a common use of **to iu** (in the plain form) to mean "named" or "called": unlike the typical English pattern, a passive is not necessary here. Thus "an American called Joe" is *Jō to iu Amerikajin*.

Finally, we remind you that *-i* adjectives in particular act verbally and effectively include the copula within themselves. Thus *takai hon* can be translated not only as "an expensive book" but "a book which is expensive." We don't often use this sort of construction in English, but it is worth noting since it indicates that the pre-noun adjective here is in fact a one-word subordinate clause in its own right, just like *katta hon* for "a book which someone bought."

LIST 6a: Recap of useful new words in 6.1

oyogimasu	to swim
kashimasu	to lend
kachimasu	to win
shinimasu	to die
kaimasu	to buy
yobimasu	to call
nomimasu	to drink
urimasu	to sell
kirimasu	to cut
hen na	strange, odd
mondai	problem

6.2 More structures

This book is not intended to be a textbook or grammar book per se, but more a description of how the Japanese language works. As part of this description we will show you a range of structures below, again at a level somewhat higher than beginner's, but we will not go into them in great detail. Most of the structures are, not surprisingly, verbal and/or adjectival.

6.2.1 The useful -*te* form (continuous tenses, giving and receiving, requests, joining verbs and adjectives)

One of the most useful forms, central to a number of structures, is the *-te* form, which is closest to the English "-ing." It is formed by replacing the final *-a* of the affirmative past plain tense (see Tables 6a and 6b) with *-e*, thus giving *tabete* ("eating"), *kaite* ("writing"), *yonde* ("reading") etc.

It has a variety of uses, including as a verbal participle. This gives a range of continuous tenses, as in "I am/was reading." Again like English, it also requires an auxiliary verb, but unlike English, which uses either "to be" or "to have," it takes only one, *iru*/*imasu*. Thus "I am/was reading an interesting book" is (*Watashi wa*) *omoshiroi hon o yonde imasu*/*imashita*, etc. With certain verbs, involving motion or change of state, this becomes more like "has -ed/-en." For instance, *ochite imasu* (*ochimasu* means "to fall") can mean "is falling" but usually means "has fallen," while the *-te* form of *narimasu* ("to become"), *natte imasu*, almost always means "has become." It can also mean, depending on the context, "have been ...-ing," as in *Kyonen kara benkyō shite imasu* ("I have been studying since last year").

Similarly, note how *-te imasen* sometimes corresponds to "I have not ...ed." For example, using *mō* meaning "yet" or "now/by now" and *mada* with the negative meaning "not yet," we could have the following exchange:

Watashi no hon o mō yomimashita ka ("Have you read my book yet?")
Ie, mada yonde imasen ("No, I haven't read it yet.")

The *-te* form acts more like a gerund (a verbal noun, as in "reading broadens the mind") when used of doing actions for others, as we outlined in 6.1.1. Thus you offer up a doing of an action to others, while others bestow the doing of an action upon you. The most common word for "to offer up" is *agemasu*, and "to bestow/give down" is *kuremasu*, while "to bestow" from a particularly high status is *kudasaimasu*. In their simplest usage these can be used directly with simple nouns, as in *Tomodachi ni hon o agemashita* ("I gave my friend a book"), *Tomodachi wa hon o kuremashita* ("My friend gave me a book"), and *Sensei wa hon o kudasaimashita* ("The teacher gave me a book").

The same structure applies to actions, with a gerund replacing the simple noun. Thus, using *kashimasu* meaning "to lend," we could say *Tomodachi ni pen o kashite agemashita* ("I lent my friend a pen"). Note the use of *ni* here. Similarly we could say *Tomodachi wa pen o kashite kuremashita* ("My friend lent me a pen"). And using *setsumei shimasu* for "to explain" and *bunpō* for "grammar," we could say *Sensei wa Nihongo no bunpō o setsumei shite kudasaimashita*, meaning "The teacher explained Japanese grammar (to me)."

Phrased from the recipient's perspective, you can use a verb **moraimasu** meaning "to receive," or **itadakimasu** for a person of particularly high status, thus **Tomodachi ni pen o kashite moraimashita** and **Sensei ni setsumei shite itadakimashita**. (Note again the use of **ni**, this time, rather confusingly, having a meaning similar to the English "from" rather than "to.")

Another use of this concept of bestowing an action is to make a request. To ask for a loan of five dollars you could ask **Godoru kashite kure-masen ka**, which is equivalent to something like "Won't you lend me five dollars?" and might be appropriate among acquaintances. (...**te ku-dasaimasen ka** would be more appropriate among non-acquaintances.) Alternatively you could make a straightout direct request, "Please lend me five dollars." In the latter case we use an imperative form of **kuda-saimasu**, namely **kudasai**. Thus **Godoru kashite kudasai**. (And note in passing that **o** is not needed with an expression of quantity.)

Also in passing we should say that a less polite imperative, commonly used in neutral situations such as exam instructions but which we sug-gest you don't employ too much yourself, uses a structure (**o** +) verb stem + **nasai**. The verb stem is what is left when you remove **-masu**. Thus the clinical instruction "Write your name" ("name" is **namae**) would be **Namae o kaki-nasai**. If **nasai** is replaced by **kudasai**, e.g. **O-namae o kaki-kudasai**, it becomes much politer, such as a salesperson might use of a client. We suggest, however, that you stick with **-te kuda-sai** (e.g. **O-namae o kaite kudasai**). (Remember the polite prefix **o-**.)

(You might also hear the very brusque form of the imperative, which is made by replacing the **-u** of **-u** verbs with **-e** and the **-ru** of **-ru** verbs with **-ro**. Thus **Yome** for "Read it!" and **Tabero** for "Eat it!" The negative rather confusingly takes **na** after an affirmative present plain form, thus **Sonna koto suru na** means "Don't do that!" Do not use these forms yourself. And note too that **o** can be omitted in such cases.)

Yet another use of the **-te** form is for seeking permission. The request uses the **-te** form plus the particle **mo**, here used in its adverbial sense of "even," to give something like "Even doing such and such a thing, is it okay?" Thus to say "May I go?" you would say **Itte mo ii desu ka**. Hope-fully your wish will be granted and the answer will be (**Itte mo**) **ii desu yo**.

Another important use we will introduce here for the **-te** form is its conjunctive role. That is, it joins verbal or adjectival clauses. Thus "Mary came at five o'clock and went home at six" would be ***Mearii-san wa goji ni kite, rokuji ni uchi ni kaerimashita*** (***uchi*** means "home"). If you wish to emphasize the sequence, you can use **kara** after the **-te** form. Thus, using **kenka shimasu** ("to quarrel"), you could say **Kenka shite kara uchi ni kaerimashita**, meaning "I went home after quarrelling." (Note how this differs from **kara** after other forms, where it means "so" [see 5.4.2]: as e.g. **Kenka shita (/shi-mashita) kara uchi ni kaerimashita**, meaning "I went home because we quarrelled.")

Adjectives have a **-te** form too, **-kute** replacing the final **i** for **-i** adjectives and **de** for **na** adjectives—**de** being the **-te** form of the copula. Thus, using **tenki** for "weather," we might say **Hijō ni atsukute, iya na tenki deshita** ("It was extremely hot and unpleasant weather").

There is a negative **-te** form, or more exactly two in the case of verbs. The first is **-nakute**, which replaces the **-nai** of the plain negative (or in the case of **-i** adjectives, the whole **nai**, e.g. **atsuku nai** goes to **atsuku nakute**). This is used when seeking permission. Thus **Ikanakute mo ii desu ka** is how you would ask "Is it all right if I don't go?"

The other form for verbs uses **-naide** instead of **nakute**. This is used in the **-te kudasai** direct request, thus **Nanimo iwanaide kudasai** ("Please don't say anything" [remember the negative of **iu** is **iwanai**]).

Either form can be used as a conjunctive, but neither is used in the continuative tense structures, for it is the auxiliary that changes. That is, "I wasn't watching" is not **Minaide/minakute imashita** but **Mite imasen deshita**.

Finally, the **-te** form is often used with a handful of particular verbs to form a sort of compound idea. One common example is with **shimaimasu**, a verb meaning "to put something away" or "to finish off." When used after a **-te** form it means to do something thoroughly or to end up doing it against your better judgment. Thus **Kēki o zenbu tabete shimaimashita** means "I ended up eating the whole cake." Two other common examples are **-te mimasu**, which means "try doing something" and which we will discuss in the next section, and **-te okimasu**, which means "do something in advance" (by way of preparation, or sometimes to get it out of the way), such as *Biiru o katte okimashita* ("I bought some beer in").

6.2.2 Suggesting, probability, and trying

Suggesting something in Japanese is easy, especially at the *-masu* level, for you simply replace the *-masu* with *-mashō*. Thus *Ikimashō ka* means "Shall we go?", to which a positive reply ("Yes, let's go") would be *Ē, ikimashō*.

As with English, this tense is also used of the first person singular in the case of wondering whether you should do something, equivalent to "Shall I go?" When talking or thinking to yourself it would be unnatural to use a *-masu* form. The plain form is made in the case of *-ru* verbs by replacing the *-ru* with *-yō*, and in the case of *-u* verbs by replacing the *-u* with *-ō*. (Note the irregular *suru* goes to *shiyō*.) Thus *Ikō kana, Tabeyō kana, Shiyō kana*, etc. (The "wondering" particle *kana* is more normal than just *ka* in this case.)

But unlike English, it is also quite often used of the first person singular without it being a question, but more in the sense of "I might (per-haps)." In this case it is followed by the quotative particle *to* and the verb *omou/omoimasu*, meaning "to think." Thus *Ashita ikō to omotte imasu* means "I'm thinking I might go tomorrow," or even simply "I think I will go tomorrow."

Another use of *ō* + *to* is with *shimasu* instead of *omoimasu*. This gives the idea of trying to do something. Thus, using *ji* meaning a letter (as in print), we might say *Yomō to shimashita keredomo, ji ga chiisakute, dame deshita*, meaning "I tried to read (it), but the print was too small and (so) it was hopeless."

Do not confuse the above "try to" in the sense of "endeavor" with the idea of trying something to see what happens. The latter is formed by the *-te* form followed by *mimasu* ("to see"). Thus *Yonde mimashita keredomo, amari omoshiroku arimasen deshita* means "I tried reading (it) but it wasn't very interesting."

The *-mashō* form of the copula *desu* is *deshō* (*darō* in the plain form). It is usually equivalent to "probably" or "I dare say," and can be used by itself or following a plain form (affirmative or negative). Thus *Hiroshi-san wa gakusei deshō* ("Hiroshi's probably a student"), *Sensei wa ikanai deshō* ("The teacher probably won't go"), and *Takai deshō* ("I dare say it's expensive").

Deshō is used quite a lot as it is considered softer and more indirect than a straightforward *desu*, in similar fashion to polite English speakers who will choose to say something like "I think this may be wrong" or "This is perhaps wrong" rather than the blunter "This is wrong."

Whereas *deshō* indicates probability, the sentence-ending term *ka mo shiremasen* (literally "one cannot know whether...") indicates mere possibility. Thus *Hiroshi-san wa gakusei ka mo shiremasen* (note that the copula can be omitted entirely) means "Hiroshi possibly may be a student," and *Sensei wa ikanai ka mo shiremasen* means "The teacher possibly may not go."

6.2.3 If and when, must and mustn't
There are various ways of saying "if," perhaps the most useful being the *-tara* form. This simply requires *-ra* to be added to the past plain tense of both verbs and adjectives (both affirmative and negative, the latter giving *-nakattara*). Thus, using *mushi* meaning "insect," we might say *Kono hen na mushi o tabetara* (/*tabete mitara*), *modosu deshō*, meaning "If you ate (/tried eating) this weird bug, you'd probably throw up." As another example, *Muzukashikattara, shinakute mo ii desu yo* means "If it's difficult, you don't have to do it." *Na* adjectives take the *-tara* form of the copula, *dattara*. Thus *Iya dattara, tabenakute mo ii desu yo* means "If you don't like it, you don't have to eat it."

There is another way of expressing the *-tara* form of the copula, and that is *nara*. We could, for example, have said *iya nara* above. It can follow the plain form of verbs and adjectives (both affirmative and negative), and so it is quite useful. In particular, it is used in conditions such as in response to something someone has said (or something you've learned about), not unlike "Well, if it's the case that..., then..." It is also the form to use in cases where the action in the "if clause" occurs later than the other action, e.g. "If you're going to study Japanese, please read this book [first]" ("first" is *mazu*): *Nihongo o benkyō suru nara*, [*mazu*] *kono hon o yonde kudasai*.

-Tara (but not *nara*) can sometimes mean "when" rather than "if." For example, using *sagasu/sagashimasu* meaning "to search for," we might say *Sagashite mitara, asoko ni arimashita*, which would translate as "When I tried looking for it, there it was."

Another way of expressing "if" is to use the *-eba* form. This replaces the final *-u* of the plain present, for both *-u* verbs and *-ru* verbs. It tends to have an implication that doing the action to which *-eba* applies is a condition for whatever follows to come about. Thus *Kore o yomeba wakarimasu* means "If you read this then you'll understand." Or, using the bug example from above, if we said *Kono hen na mushi o tabereba, modoshimasu*, then it would imply you wanted to throw up and we were suggesting a probable way of satisfying that desire.

(The *-tara* and *-eba* forms are often seen as interchangeable. Sometimes that is true in practice, but in addition to the difference in focus mentioned above, technically *-eba* should not be used if there is any subjectivity in the main clause, such as for example if we had said *wakaru deshō* instead of just *wakarimasu* in the above example.)

Affirmative *-i* adjectives form *-eba* in similar fashion to negative verbs, and that is by having the final *-i* replaced by *-kereba*: thus *atsukereba* etc. The negative is *atsuku nakereba*. Affirmative *na* adjectives take *de areba* (or a form *naraba*), negatives *de nakereba*.

There is a fixed expression *-nakereba narimasen* that means "must" (literally "if such-and-such an action isn't done then things won't work out"). That is, *Kore o yomanakereba narimasen* means "You must read this." Note that this is not used in the positive as a prohibition: that is, you cannot say *yomeba narimasen* to mean "mustn't read." Rather, the *-te* form is used with a term like *dame desu* or *ikemasen* (this is actually a potential form of *ikimasu*, here meaning "to be acceptable". We will discuss potentials in a later section). So, to say "You mustn't eat that" is *Sore o tabete wa dame desu* or *Sore o tabete wa ikemasen*.

There is a structurally very simple way of expressing both "if" and "when," particularly in the case of causal generalizations (i.e. "whenever"), and that is to add a particle *to* (not the quotative or conjunctive, but a third *to*!) to the plain present form. We might, for example, say

Ame ga furu to, tenisu o shimasen. This would translate as "We don't play play tennis if/when(ever) it rains." It doesn't have to be a generalization. For example, using the *-u* verb *hairu/hairimasu* meaning to "enter," we could say *Heya ni hairu to, terebi ga arimashita* ("When I went into the room, there was a television"). The causality is there in that it was only when I entered the room that I became aware of the television. Note *to* cannot follow a past tense, even though it may be used in a past tense sentence.

Finally, a way of categorically saying "when" as opposed to "if" is to follow the plain form (past or present, negative or affirmative) of a verb or adjective with the word *toki*, meaning "(point in) time." Thus, "When (/at the time) I went went to France I was a student" is *Furansu ni itta toki (wa) gakusei deshita*.

6.2.4 Seeming

One of the most common ways of expressing "like" or "seeming" is to use the *na* adjective *yō na*. *Yō* exists as a noun meaning "manner" or "way," but is rarely used independently. Instead it is used for example with demonstrative adjectives, such as *kono yō na* meaning "this manner of" (very similar to *konna*), or adverbially *kono yō ni* meaning "in this way"/"like this." When following a noun it takes *no*, thus *Furansu-jin no yō na hito*. This can mean either "people who look like they're French," or "people such as the French." It can also follow the plain form of a noun or adjective: thus *Maiku-san wa kinō kita yō desu* means "It seems/looks like Mike came yesterday" (i.e. inference).

Having a similar meaning of "-like" is *-mitai*—which is actually a *na* adjective. This can act as a direct noun suffix (i.e. not requiring *no*), thus *raion-mitai na neko* for "a lion-like cat"/"a cat that looks like a lion." (It is also possible to say *raion no yō na neko*.) *Mitai* can also be used as an independent word, such as (*Sō*) *mitai desu* for "It looks that way/It looks like that's the case," or *Kinō kita mitai desu* ("It seems he came yesterday").

Whereas both *yō* and *mitai* can be used of both conjecture and appearance, the word *rashii* has a different application (though often confused by foreigners in practice). It refers to reported speech (or similar), and also to typicality. Thus *Kinō kita rashii desu* would mean more specifically "I hear he's come." You could not say *raion rashii neko*, but you could say *neko rashii neko* meaning "a cat-like (/typical) cat," while the statement *Neko rashii desu nē* could mean something like "How typical of a cat!" *Furansujin rashii desu* could mean either "How French-like he/she is" or "I hear he/she's French."

Finally, two items that are often confused are *sō desu* meaning "it is said that" and the suffix *-sō desu* meaning "looking like" (purely of appearance). The former follows a plain form (including *da*): thus *Kinō kita sō desu* for "They say he came yesterday." The latter is actually a *na* adjectival suffix, and goes on to the stem of a verb or adjective. Thus, *kane ga arisō na hito* means "a person who looks to have (a lot of) money."

A clear illustration of the difference is seen in:

Afurika wa atsui sō desu: "They say that Africa's hot."
Afurika wa atsusō desu: "Africa looks like it's hot." (e.g. you comment as you are watching a video of a drought).

6.2.5 Purpose and cause
You have already seen in 5.4.1 one way of expressing purpose when motion is involved, namely "stem plus *ni* plus verb of motion" (*eiga o mi ni ikimasu*).

Another easy way of expressing purpose, regardless of whether motion is involved or not, is simply to add *tame* (*ni*) to the plain form of a verb. Thus "I'm studying Japanese (in order) to become a teacher" is *Sensei ni naru tame ni Nihongo o benkyō shite imasu*.

Tame ni as a purpose indicator is fine if the subject is the same in both the main clause and the purpose clause, and if no potentiality is involved. If the subjects differ, or if potentiality is involved, *yō ni* should be used instead. (This is the same *yō* as in the previous section, but in a different usage.) As an example in which subjects differ, using *mensetsu* meaning "interview" and *junbi shimasu* meaning "to prepare," along with the phrase *umaku iku* meaning "to go well," we could say *Mensetsu ga umaku iku yō ni junbi shite imasu* ("I'm preparing so that my interview will go well"). We will introduce potentials presently, but you are already partly familiar with one potential verb, ***dekiru/dekimasu*** meaning "to be able/possible." Thus, using **unten** meaning "driving" and **renshū shimasu** meaning "to practice," we could say **Unten ga dekiru yō ni renshū shite imasu** ("I'm practicing so that I can drive"). You can see here, from the particle **ga**, that technically **unten** becomes the subject of the purpose clause, whereas "I am" is a different subject in the main clause, and hence the rule applies that **tame** should not be used.

Tame is still a very useful word because, like the English term "on account of," it can be used to explain cause as well as purpose. It either follows the plain form of a verb or adjective, or a noun plus **no**. Thus, using ***ame ga furu/furimasu*** meaning literally "rain falls," "I didn't go because of (/on account of) the rain" would be **Ame no tame ikimasen deshita** or **Ame ga futte ita tame ikimasen deshita**. Note that **ni** is commonly dropped when using **tame** for cause rather than purpose.

Remember that you have already encountered one way of expressing cause in 5.4.2 and 6.2.1, and that is **kara** meaning "so": **Kenka shita kara uchi ni kaerimashita** ("I went home because we quarreled").

We also touched earlier in passing (5.4.2) upon the term **no de**, which can function instead of **kara** when a cause is factual, such as for example **Ame ga futte ita no de ikimasen deshita**. This in fact is a suspensive form of **no desu**—often abbreviated to **-n desu**—which is similar to the English expression "the thing is that..." This is often used at the end of a sentence, after a plain form, to justify actions, i.e. as a sort of causal explanation, or to add further information about a situation with which the other party was partly familiar. For example, using **isogashii** meaning "busy" and **hontō ni** meaning "truly"/"really," you might justify declining an invitation to go out somewhere by saying **Kyō wa hontō ni isogashiin desu (kedo)**... ("The thing is, I'm really busy today..."). Or, if your friend saw you walking to work and looked puzzled, because you always drove and he/she knew that (i.e. it is shared knowledge), you might say, using **kuruma** for "car" and **koshō shimasu** for "to break down," **Kuruma ga koshō shitan desu** ("The thing is, you see, my car broke down").

6.2.6 Comparison and ought/should

Comparison is another matter that is not very difficult to express in Japanese. A key word is *hō*, which means "side" or "direction" or "option" in the sense of "selection from amongst a range." *Yasui hō no doresu o kaimashita*, for example, is similar to the English "I bought a dress on the cheap side," while *Kono doresu no hō ga kirei desu* means "This dress is prettier (than the other)."

In this sense *hō* is usually used of a comparison between two items (i.e. comparatively, as "-er"). A typical question might be *Orenji to ringo to (de wa), dochira (no hō ga) yasui desu ka* ("Which is the cheaper, oranges or apples?"). Note the use here of the particles *to* (meaning "and") and *de* (meaning "among"). If it were apples, then you could say *Ringo no hō ga yasui desu*. If more than two are involved (i.e. superlatively, as "-est"), then the adverb *ichiban* ("most," literally meaning "number one") is used. Thus, if choosing from a range of dresses, you could say *Kono doresu ga ichiban kirei desu* ("This is the prettiest dress").

To express the word "than" in a comparison, as in "Spain is hotter than Iceland," *yori* is used after the lesser item. Thus, depending on your focus, you could say *Aisurando yori Supein no hō ga atsui desu* (if Iceland was your main focus) or *Supein wa Aisurando yori atsui desu* (if Spain was your main focus).

In a negative comparison, namely "Iceland isn't as hot as Spain," the word *hodo* (literally "extent") is used, giving *Aisurando wa Supein hodo atsuku arimasen/atsuku nai desu*. To make a statement of equality, a different word *kurai/gurai* (also meaning "extent") is used, usually with the irregular adjective (*to*) *onaji* (meaning "the same"), giving *Porutogaru wa Supein to onaji gurai atsui desu* ("Portugal is as hot as Spain").

Returning to *hō*, when used after a plain form, and with a suitable adjective—usually *ii*/"good"—it can mean "it's better to do such-and-such a thing," which can also sometimes translate as "ought" or "should." A past tense is often used here of the plain form, largely stylistically. For example, *Hayaku iku hō ga ii desu* means "It's better to go quickly," whereas *Hayaku itta hō ga ii desu* means "It would be better to go quickly"/"We should (/ought to) go quickly." A negative is also possible, as in *Ikanai hō ga ii desu* ("It's better not to go").

The *-tara* form can also be used in some "ought"/"should" situations. For example, **Dō shitara ii ka wakarimasen** (literally "I don't know if in which way I acted it would be good") would be a way of saying "I don't know what I should do"/"I don't know what I ought to do." (Note how **dō** is used here: **nani o** is also possible.) A reply might be **Hayashi-sensei to hanashite mitara dō desu ka** ("What about if you tried talking to Professor Hayashi?"/"You could try talking to Professor Hayashi").

Another way of saying "ought" or "should," this time more in the sense of expectation than suggestion (i.e. "Bill ought to have arrived by now"), is to use **hazu** after a plain form. Using the adverb **mō** (meaning "by now") and **tsukimasu** meaning "to arrive," we could express our example as **Biru-san wa mō tsuita (/tsuite iru) hazu desu**. A negative equivalent, using the adverb **mada** ("not yet"), would be **Mada tsuite inai hazu desu** ("He won't have arrived yet"). A simpler way of saying more or less the same thing in both cases would be to use **deshō** instead of **hazu desu**.

6.2.7 Potentials, passives, and causatives

The simplest way of making a potential is to use the verb **dekimasu**, which in itself means "to be possible" (as well as "to be produced"). Thus, using **shigoto** meaning "work," we could say **Watashi (ni) wa konna shigoto wa (/ga) dekimasen** (literally "As for me, this sort of work is not possible") to express "I can't do this sort of work." (Note the optional use of **ni**, meaning something like "for" in this case.) Basically, almost any noun that can be used with **shimasu** can form a potential with **dekimasu**, e.g. **Setsumei dekimasu** ("I can explain"). When used with a verb rather than a noun, the verb is in effect converted into a noun by adding **koto** (meaning an abstract "thing') to its plain form. For instance, using the verb **hanasu/ hanashimasu** meaning "to speak," we could say **Watashi wa Nihongo o hanasu koto ga dekimasu**, meaning "I am able to (/can) speak Japanese" (literally "As for me the speaking of Japanese is possible").

Dekimasu is very useful, but there is also a specific potential form of verbs. We used **ka mo shiremasen** earlier to mean "may" or "might." It is in fact the potential form of **shirimasu**, "to know," and literally means "one cannot know (for sure)." It is a useful expression that can be used in a more general sense. For example, **Takai ka mo shiremasen** means "It might (/could) be expensive (for all I know)."

As **shiremasen** might indicate, the potential is formed in the case of **-u** verbs by changing the **-u** to **-eru**, which then functions as a **-ru** verb. Thus, using again the verb **hanasu/hanashimasu** meaning "to speak," the potential form "able to speak" is **hanaseru/hanasemasu**.

One interesting point to note, however, is that—as suggested in fact by **koto ga dekimasu** above—the object particle for a regular verb becomes a subject particle when used with a potential form. Thus, whereas **Watashi wa Eigo o hanashimasu** means simply "I speak English," the potential "I can speak Japanese" is **Watashi wa Nihongo ga hanasemasu**. It's not a serious error nowadays if you say **Nihongo o hanasemasu**, but technically **ga** is correct. (Actually, the same applies with the verb **wakarimasu** meaning "to understand." This has "built in" potentiality, so it is correct to say **Watashi wa Nihongo ga wakarimasu**.)

In the case of **-ru** verbs, the potential is formed by replacing **-ru** with **-rareru** (itself a **-ru** verb ending). Thus **taberu/tabemasu** goes to **taberareru/taberaremasu**, giving **Watashi wa washoku** (="Japanese-style food") **ga taberaremasu** for "I can eat Japanese food." Young people nowadays often abbreviate this form by removing **ra**, thus giving **tabereru/taberemasu**—in effect, treating **-ru** verbs as **-u** verbs.

The above phrase **washoku ga taberaremasu**, meaning literally "Japanese food is able to be eaten (by me)," overlaps conceptually with the passive. The potential ending for **-ru** verbs, **-rareru**, is in fact one and the same as the passive form of **-ru** verbs. As another example, **Koko de mirareru yō ni**... can be translated as "As is seen here..." or "As can be seen here..." or "As we can see here" The overlap between "can be" and "is" in English shows that English too has a similar conceptualization. And note that, as we touched upon in 6.2.5 in the discussion of purpose, the potential is used with **yō ni** rather than **tame ni**, so this same sentence could also mean "So that we can see."

Unfortunately the same full overlap does not apply so neatly to **-u** verbs. Whereas the potential form replaces **-u** with **-eru**, the passive replaces **-u** with **-areru**. Thus "This is widely (=**hiroku**) known" is **Kore wa hiroku shirarete imasu**, and "It is often said" is **Yoku iwarete imasu**. (Note again the use of the glide **w** after a vowel, as **iarete** would be hard to pronounce.)

As with English, Japanese has both direct passives and indirect passives. The former is seen in a sentence such as "My money was stolen," the latter in "I had my money stolen." The verb "to steal" is ***nusumimasu***, and in Japanese these would be ***Watashi no o-kane ga nusumaremashita*** and ***Watashi wa o-kane o nusumaremashita*** respectively. The indirect passive can also be used of intransitive verbs (i.e. verbs that normally do not take an object), such as "to come." In English we can say "I had a visitor come" in the sense of having them descend on us unexpectedly and causing a bit of inconvenience. (In fact, the indirect passive in Japanese usually indicates some sort of annoyance or suffering.) The same sense can be conveyed in Japanese using ***koraremasu***, the irregular passive (and potential) of ***kuru***: (***Watashi wa***) ***o-kyakusan ni koraremashita***. Note the use of ***ni***, and note how this example is stronger than the one used used earlier regarding ***ga***: ***Tomodachi ga kimashita***, meaning simply "A friend came." The passive of ***suru***, like ***kuru***, is irregular—***sareru***.

Another less common way of forming the passive, normally used only of inanimate items, uses the ***-te*** form with ***arimasu***. This indicates that something has been done intentionally. For example, there is a pair of verbs ***akimasu*** meaning "to open" (intransitive) and ***akemasu*** "to open" (transitive). Using ***mado*** meaning "window," we could say ***Mado wa aite imasu***, meaning simply "The window is open." By contrast, ***Mado wa akete arimasu*** means "The window has been opened"/"Someone has opened the window (for a purpose, and left it in that state)."

Another verbal form is the causative, which involves making or letting someone do something. This is formed in Japanese in similar fashion to the passive, but with ***-(s)aseru*** rather than ***-(r)areru***. That is, ***-u*** verbs have the final ***-u*** replaced by ***-aseru*** (which functions thereafter as a ***-ru*** verb), and ***-ru*** verbs have the final ***-ru-*** replaced by ***-saseru*** (again a ***-ru*** verb). The person who is made or allowed to do something is followed by ***ni***. Thus "The teacher made (/let) the students write kanji" would be ***Sensei wa gakusei ni kanji o kakasemashita***, and "The doctor made my younger brother drink a lot of water" would be ***Isha wa otōto ni mizu o takusan nomasemashita***.

The causative is often used in various higher levels of politeness when making a request, using verbs of bestowing and receiving (the latter in the potential form). For example, instead of asking directly **Yonde mo ii desu ka** ("May I read it?"), it is politer to say **Yomasete kuremasen ka** ("Won't you allow me to read it?"), politer still to say **Yomasete itadakemasu ka** ("Is it possible for me to be allowed to read it?"), and even politer still to say **Yomasete itadakenai deshō ka** ("Would it not perhaps be possible for me to be allowed to read it?"). Of course, if necessary we can make such distinctions in English, as per the translations, but this is rarer in English than it is in Japanese.

It is possible to combine passives and causatives, as in for example "My brother was made to drink a lot of water by the doctor." In such cases the final **-ru** of the causative becomes **-rareru**, so **nomaseru/nomasemasu** becomes **nomaserareru/nomaseraremasu**. Moreover, the **ni** shifts position to come after the causer of the action, i.e. the doctor: **Otōto wa isha ni mizu o takusan nomaseraremashita**. As you can imagine, this is quite a mouthful, and optional shortened forms have evolved in many cases. Just as we saw a shortening with the potential of **-ru** verbs, so too you can use here a shorter form of the causative passive, **nomasaremasu** instead of **nomaseraremasu**.

6.2.8 Miscellaneous structures
We finish this chapter on more advanced usage with a brief assortment of structures.

Desideratives: The desiderative form of a verb ("I want to...") is formed by adding **-tai** to the stem, giving **yomitai**, **tabetai** etc. The finished product then becomes an **-i** adjective, and as such is usually preceded by the subject particle **ga** or **wa**, though **o** is also possible. For example, using **naraimasu** meaning "to learn," to say "I want to learn Japanese" we might say **Nihongo ga naraitai desu** or **Nihongo ga naraitai to omoimasu** (the latter is somewhat politer, similar to "I should like to."). If we use **ga**, it focuses on "Japanese," whereas if we use **o** (**Nihongo o naraitai desu**), then it puts the focus rather on the verb. As an example of a negative, we might say **Ikitaku arimasen** for "I don't want to go."

This form is not used terribly often by Japanese people themselves, who tend to use structures such as the **-ō to omotte imasu** discussed in 6.2.2. Certainly it is usually avoided in questions other than among intimates, since it is considered rude to ask so directly about a person's desire. (So, for something like "Would you like something to drink?" one would say **Nanika nomimasu ka**.) Nor, strictly speaking, should **-tai desu** be used of third persons, though **-tai to omotte** (**/itte**) **imasu** is acceptable. Thus "John would like to go" is **Jon-san wa ikitai to omotte** (**/itte**) **imasu**.

We should also point out, as one of the interesting features of Japanese, that when adjectives of a clearly subjective nature, such as those expressing volition or desire, are used of a third person, then they can actually become verbs in which the final **-i** is replaced by **-garu/-garimasu**. The **-tai** form is one such case. Thus we could have said **Jon-san wa ikitagatte imasu** to express the same idea of "John wants to go." This can even be applied to adjectives such as **omoshiroi** ("interesting"), so to say "John finds Japanese interesting" we could say either **Jon-san wa Nihongo ga omoshiroi to omotte imasu** or **Jon-san wa Nihongo o omoshirogatte imasu**.

While: Adding **-nagara** to the verb stem gives the idea of the same subject doing one action while also doing another. Thus, using **unten shimasu** meaning "to drive" and **o kikimasu** meaning "to listen to" (**ni kikimasu** means rather "to ask someone"), we could say **Unten shinagara rajio o kiite imashita** to express "I was listening to the radio as I was driving."

When different subjects are involved, Japanese uses **aida** (meaning literally "period" or "interval') or **aida ni**. The former means "during" and indicates that both actions occupy the same time, while the latter is used when the second action is shorter, and is completed within the time frame for the first action. Thus, using the verb **nemasu** meaning "to sleep," we could illustrate the former by **Watashi ga terebi o mite iru aida, neko ga/wa nete imashita** ("While I was watching TV the cat was asleep [the whole time]"). (Note the verb preceding **aida** is always in the present tense.) As an illustration of the latter, using **nezumi** for "mouse" and **nigemasu** for "to escape," we could say **Neko ga nete iru aida ni nezumi ga/wa nigemashita** ("The mouse escaped while the cat slept").

Before and after: We've seen earlier that **sanji jippun mae** means "ten minutes to three" or "ten minutes before three." **Mae** can also be used after a plain present, to give for example (using **te** "hand" and **araimasu** "to wash") **Taberu mae ni te o araimashō** ("Let's wash our hands before we eat": note **ni**). It can also be used directly after a word indicating a period of time, such as **Sanjūgonen mae kara Nihongo o naratte imasu** ("I have been learning Japanese since 35 years ago"), and it can follow a noun plus **no**, as in **sensō no mae ni** ("before the war").

We've already seen too that "after doing something" can be expressed by **-te kara**, e.g. **Shukudai o owatte kara terebi o mimashita** ("I watched TV after finishing my homework"). Another way of saying this is past plain plus **ato**, thus **Shukudai o owatta ato (de) terebi o mimashita**. **Ato** can follow directly after a word indicating period of time, such as **sankagetsu ato (ni/de)**, meaning "after three months," or it can follow a noun plus **no**, as **arashi no ato de** meaning "after the storm."

Only: There are several ways of expressing "only." One is to use **dake** after the item. Thus **Tomodachi dake ga kimashita** means "Only my friend(s) came." Another is to use **bakari**. After a noun this acts not unlike **dake**. "Mike only watches Westerns (**seibugeki**)" is **Maiku-san wa seibugeki bakari (o) mite imasu**. However, unlike **dake**, **bakari** can shift the focus. The example above implies that, when watching films, Mike only watches Westerns. By contrast, if we wanted to say Mike spends all his time watching Westerns, we can reposition **bakari** to give **Maiku-san wa seibugeki o mite bakari imasu**. Another way of saying "only" is **shika** plus the negative, similar to the English "nothing but" or "none but," though it also often carries an implication that what is expressed is below the speaker's expectation. Thus **Kore shika dekimasen deshita** ("I could only manage this"/"I couldn't do any more than just this").

"Easy to...", "hard to...", "way of...", "overdo": there are a number of suffixes that can be added to verb stems to give a particular meaning. For example, **-yasui** can have a meaning of "easy to" when used as a suffix, so **Kore wa yomiyasui hon desu** means "This is an easy-to-read book." There are a number of suffixes to express "hard to," but one of the commonest is **-nikui**, such as in for example **wakarinikui** meaning "hard to understand." The addition of **-kata**, by contrast, gives the idea of "way of doing something." Thus, a "strange way of walking" would be **hen na arukikata**. And **shikata**, meaning literally "way of doing (something)," features in the common saying **Shikata ga nai (/arimasen)**, meaning "There's nothing that can be done about it." The addition of *-sugiru* (a *-ru* verb), which as an independent verb means "to exceed," gives a meaning of overdoing something, as in **nomisugimasu** for "to drink too much." It can also be applied to adjectives, such as **Kore wa takasugimasu** meaning "This is too expensive."

Whether and indirect questions: To express something like "I don't know whether John will go to America (or not)" we would say **Jon-san ga Amerika ni iku ka (dō ka) wakarimasen**. (Note the use of **dō ka** here, and note too the use of **wakarimasen**: **shirimasen** would mean rather "I don't know and I don't care.") **Atsui ka samui ka wakarimasen** means "I can't tell (/I don't know) if it's hot or cold."

Indirect questions make for fairly sophisticated Japanese, as they do also in English. For example, "If you try studying kanji, I think you'll soon (**sugu**) appreciate just how difficult they are to remember (**oboemasu**)" would be in Japanese: **Kanji o benkyō shite mitara, donna ni oboenikui ka sugu wakaru to omoimasu**.

If you can handle this level of Japanese, you're doing more than okay! It doesn't get very much more complex, apart from the finer points of respect language, which we discuss next in 6.3. First, let us recap in List 6b some of the useful words that have cropped up in illustrations in the course of this long sub-chapter 6.2.

LIST 6b: Recap of useful new words in 6.2

ochimasu	to fall
agemasu	to offer, lift up
kuremasu	to give down, bestow
kudasaimasu	to bestow from high status
itadakimasu	to receive
moraimasu	to receive
setsumei	explanation
bunpō	grammar
ringo	apple
namae	name
tenki	weather
omoimasu	to think
ji	letter (of print)

mushi	insect, bug
sagashimasu	to search
mensetsu	interview
junbi	preparation
unten	driving
renshū	practice
ame	rain
furimasu	to fall (of rain etc.)
warui	bad
isogashii	busy
kuruma	vehicle, car
koshō shimasu	to break down (car etc.)
hontō ni	truly, really
tsukimasu	to arrive
shigoto	work
hanashimasu	to speak
washoku	Japanese food
wakarimasu	to understand
hiroku	widely
nusumimasu	to steal
akimasu	to open (v.i.)
akemasu	to open (v.t.)
mado	window
mizu	water
naraimasu	to learn
unten	driving
rajio	radio
kikimasu	to listen
nemasu	to sleep
nezumi	mouse
nigemasu	to escape
te	hand
araimasu	to wash
arashi	storm
seibugeki	a Western (film)
sugu	straightaway
oboemasu	to memorize

6.3 Respect language

We have already seen quite a bit of how to express politeness (or not) in Japanese. In this sub-chapter we go a little further and introduce what is known as **keigo** ("respect language"). The core principle of humbling yourself (and associates) and elevating others remains the same.

Language items or structures used to humble yourself are called "depreciatory." Those which elevate the status of another party, usually through the verb applied to the actions of that party, are called "honorific." This may or may not be the same person you are addressing. If, for example, you are talking about the Emperor, you will use honorific language of him and his actions whether or not you are talking to your spouse or your boss at work. In Japanese you would, however, express yourself in different politeness levels between your spouse and your boss, and the level you choose (the register) is a domain sometimes called "deferential" at higher politeness levels.

One key way of expressing differences in status is to modify verb structure. This can be applied to almost any verb (other than the special cases listed in Table 6c below). We will stay in the **-masu** form to illustrate this.

For example, using **to hanashimasu** meaning "to speak with," the standard way to say "I spoke with a friend" is (**Watashi wa**) **tomodachi to hanashimashita**, but if you were depreciating yourself you could use **o** + stem + **shimasu**, or, depreciating yourself even lower, **o** + stem + **itashimasu**, giving (**Watashi wa**) **sensei to o-hanashi shimashita** (**/itashimashita**). (You wouldn't really need the **watashi wa** as the depreciatory verb would make this clear, as well as the context.)

On the other hand, if you were referring to the action of a person of high status (including the person addressed, for example), you would use a structure **o** + stem + **ni narimasu**. Thus you might say to the venerable Mr Yamashita, **Yamashita-sama**, **konna hon o o-yomi ni narimasu ka** ("Mr Yamashita, Sir, do you read this sort of book?").

For some common verbs, such as "to be," "to go" and "to do," there is a range of different terminology depending on the category. We list the main ones below in Table 6c in plain form, except for the deferentials. These, by their nature, should not normally be used in anything but the **-masu** form.

TABLE 6c: Respect terminology for common verbs

NEUTRAL	HONORIFIC	DEPRECIATORY	DEFERENTIAL
da/de aru	*de irassharu*	–	*de gozaimasu*
aru	*gozaru*	–	*gozaimasu*
iru	*irassharu**	–	*orimasu*
iku	*irassharu**	–	*mairimasu*
kuru	*irassharu**	–	*mairimasu*
suru	*nasaru*	*itasu*	–
iu	*ossharu*	–	*mooshimasu*
miru	*goran ni naru*	*haiken suru*	–
omou	–**	*zonjiru*	–
shiru	*gozonji de aru*	*zonjiru*	–
morau	–**	*itadaku*	–
ageru	–	*sashiageru*	–
kureru	*kudasaru*	–	–
taberu	*meshiagaru*	–	–
nomu	*meshiagaru*	–	–
kariru ("borrow")	–**	*haishaku suru*	–
kiku ("ask")	–**	*ukagau*	–
tazuneru ("visit")	–**	*ukagau*	–
au ("meet")	–**	*o-me-ni kakaru*	–

*There is also an older form, ***o-ide ni naru***.
Where no honorific exists, as indicated above you should use the form **o + stem + **ni naru**, e.g. for **kiku** ("to ask"), **o-kiki ni naru**.

Note that the honorifics involving **gozaru, irassharu, ossharu, kudasaru,** and **nasaru** are slightly irregular when put into the polite **-masu** form, going to **-aimasu** rather than **-arimasu**.

An example of such very polite language might be when an impeccably mannered student says to his or her teacher: **Sensei, daigaku no kurabu ga tsukutta eiga o goran ni narimashita ka? Watakushi wa kinō haiken shimashita** ("Sir/Ma'am, have you seen the film made by the University Club? I saw it yesterday."). Note that **watakushi** is a polite form of **watashi**.

There is also a deferential form for adjectives, though apart from fixed expressions it is very rarely used (much less frequently than the above verbs). In the case of **na** adjectives, this is simply the copula, thus **benri de gozaimasu**. For **-i** adjectives it is a little trickier. Those ending in **-ai** or **-oi** go to **-ō gozaimasu**, as in **takō gozaimasu** meaning "it is expensive" and **omoshirō gozaimasu** for "it is interesting," while those ending in **-ii** or **-ui** go to **-ū gozaimasu**, as in **utsukushū gozaimasu** for "it is beautiful" (from **utsukushii**) and **furū gozaimasu** meaning "it is old." The adjective may also be prefixed by **o-**, as in the standard early morning greeting **o-hayō gozaimasu** (literally "it is early").

Somewhat confusingly, the passive form can sometimes be used as a form of honorific—though rarely by non-native speakers. Thus, for example, you might find polite (especially older) people asking you **Dochira kara koraremashita ka** for "Where are you from?" Here the passive form of **kuru** is used as a respectful alternative to **irasshaimashita**. **Dochira**, incidentally, is here a politer form of **doko**, not an interrogative pronoun.

Just as certain vocabulary items can have a polite alternative, so too can they have vulgar alternatives. By "vulgar" we mean "slang" or "low-class," as opposed to depreciatory terms which are just the opposite and very polite. As just two common examples, we might cite **kuu/kuimasu**, meaning "to eat" of animals but which is occasionally used of people, and **ore** for the male first person pronoun. There are certain specific situations in which this sort of terminology is acceptable, but generally it is unwise to use it, at least until you are fully aware of the nuances of the words you are using. Hence we refrain from giving you a list here.

Having said that, it is possible to be too polite. This is called **baka-teinei**—**baka** being "fool" (**baka na** meaning foolish), and **teinei na** meaning "polite." In some cases over-the-top politeness may even be taken as sarcasm. Thus you should avoid excesses, such as using the keigo form of adjectives in everyday speech. As in all things, take your cue judiciously from appropriate native speakers.

6.4 Some common sayings

We end this part of the book with a fairly random sample of everyday greetings and civilities, some figures of speech and similar sayings, some proverbs, and one or two tongue-twisters. With your newly acquired grammatical foundation, you should have a fair idea of how these sayings are formed, which should help you to remember them. You should use a dictionary to follow up some of the vocabulary. (We, for our part, will be seeking help over our apparent obsession with frogs and buttocks!)

LIST 6c: Common sayings

GREETINGS, THANKS, AND APOLOGIES ETC.

O-hayō gozaimasu	**Good morning** (literally "It's early")
Konnichi wa	**Good day** ("This day")
Konban wa	**Good evening** ("This evening")
Hisashiburi desu ne	**It's been a while since we last met** ("It's a long interval")
Itsumo o-sewa ni natte imasu	**I'm always indebted to you** ("I'm always in your care")
O-genki desu ka	**How are you?** ("Are you well?"—used more literally than English)
O-kagesama de	**I'm well, thank you** ("Thanks to your shadow")
O-yasumi-nasai	**Good night** ("Please rest")
Sayō nara	**Goodbye** ("If it is so")
Sumimasen	**Sorry, excuse me,** often **thank you** ("[My behavior] isn't settled")
Shitsurei shimashita	**Excuse me** ("I made an impoliteness")
Arigatō (/gozaimashita)	**Thank you** ("I am humbly grateful")
Dōmo	**Thank you** or **sorry** (informal) ("In every way...")
O-negai-shimasu	**Please** (do this for me) ("I humbly request")
O-me ni kakarete kōei desu	**Honored to meet you** ("Honored to bring myself to your eyes")

Yoroshiku o-negai shimasu	**Said on first meeting** (approximate meaning "Please look upon me favourably")
Irasshai(/mase)	**Welcome** (used by shop staff) ("Come")
Yoku irasshaimashita	**Welcome** (to guests) ("Well come")

SOME FIGURES OF SPEECH

Kaeru no tsura ni mizu	**Water off a duck's back** ("water off a frog's face")
Nyōbō no shiri ni shikareru	**To be henpecked** ("to be sat upon by one's wife's buttocks")
Heso ga yadogae o suru	**To be in stitches of laughter** ("one's belly-button changes lodgings")
He o hitte shiri o tsubomeru	**Shutting the stable-door after the horse has bolted** ("clenching the buttocks after farting")
Mimi ni tako ga dekiru	**To get sick of hearing the same old thing** ("a callus forms in the ear")
Hara ga tatsu	**To get angry** ("the stomach rises")
Hanagusuri	**A bribe** ("nose medicine")
Nekobaba shita	**I quietly appropriated it** ("I acted like a cat with its droppings" [i.e. concealed the fact I'd taken it])
Neko ni koban	**To cast pearls before swine** ("coins to a cat")

PROVERBS

I no naka no kaeru taikai o shirazu	**The frog in the well knows nothing of the great ocean** (*-azu* is an old negative form of *-anai*)

Kaeru no ko wa kaeru

Like father, like son
("the frog's child is a frog")

*Inu wa mikka no on o sannen
wasurenai*

Feed a dog for three days
and he'll be grateful for
three years

Ichi o kiite jū o shiru

A word to the wise ("hear one,
know ten")

Hana yori dango

Bread not words
("dumplings rather than
flowers")

Jigoku de hotoke

An oasis in the desert
("Buddha in hell")

Nō aru taka wa tsume o kakusu

Still waters run deep ("a skilled
hawk hides its talons")

Tade kuu mushi mo sukizuki

Everyone to their taste
("even bugs that eat
knotweed have their likes")

TONGUE-TWISTERS

*Namamugi, namagome,
namatamago*

("Raw barley, raw rice, raw
eggs" [not so difficult for
English speakers!])

Tōkyō tokkyo kyoka kyoku

("the Tokyo Patent Office")

*Tonari no kyaku wa yoku kaki
kuu kyaku da*

("The visitor next door is a
visitor who eats a lot of
persimmons")

*Bōzu ga byōbu ni jōzu ni bōzu
no e o kaita*

("A priest skillfully painted
a picture of a priest on a
screen)"

*Niwa ni wa niwa, ura niwa ni mo
niwa, niwa ni mo ura niwa ni mo
niwa zutsu niwatori ga iru*

("Two in the garden, two
more in the back-garden,
so that makes two chickens
each in the garden and back-
garden")

PART FOUR

Sentences Into Script

As any language specialist knows, there are four main skills involved in language work: hearing, speaking, reading, and writing. Although so far we have necessarily had to use a form of writing—Romanization—to express in this book the Japanese sounds, words and grammar needed for hearing and speaking, this is not authentic Japanese script. In this fourth and final part we switch our focus to script proper, to give you a good idea of what reading and writing real Japanese is like.

CHAPTER SEVEN

The Writing System

Here, we give you more information on the Japanese writing system, based as it is on kanji and kana. We do not revisit Romanization.

7.1 Script components and their development

We start with a historical recap and then give you tables showing the two sets of kana systems, and their origins, and then some kanji and their origins. We also discuss uses and readings. Finally, in the next sub-chapter we give you some extensive written text, using example sentences given earlier in Romanization.

7.1.1 Recap and overview of the writing system

We have already mentioned how the Japanese writing system was developed from the adoption and adaptation of the Chinese writing system some 1,500 years ago, in order to express in written form a language that until then had existed only in spoken form. This move may have been unfortunate, as there are major structural differences between Chinese and Japanese, and Japanese might have benefited more from a straightforward alphabetic system of written representation—a form of which is seen in the phonetic kana syllabary systems that were relatively soon developed.

One reason for the adoption of Chinese characters (kanji) was that, at the time, Japan (insomuch as there was a sense of nationhood proper in those days) was an emerging state, and its leaders were keen to impress upon the leaders of a much longer established and more powerful China that they were civilized people. As it happens the writing system was actually introduced into Japan by priests from Paekche, one of the ancient kingdoms that eventually became part of present day Korea, but in those days the Korean Hangul script did not exist—that is, there was a dearth of alternative script models. The Chinese script, along with almost all things Chinese (and a few others mistakenly seen as Chinese, such as Buddhism), was a hallmark of civilization in that part of the world.

In this book we will not burden you with a detailed explanation of the various processes by which the present writing system evolved after trial and error and modification, largely in the attempt to distinguish between kanji used for their meaning and kanji used for their sound. But basically, it was the kana that were developed for phonetic purposes, leading to the present complex reality in which kanji are generally used for their meaning and to express the stem of a word, with the kana (overwhelmingly hiragana) phonetic system generally being used to express the variable endings of words along with particles and so forth.

7.1.2 The kana syllabaries

The word "kana" literally means "borrowed name," referring to their use to indicate sound. Within the kana system there are two scripts, hiragana ("common cursive kana") and katakana ("one-part kana"). Both of these were developed during the ninth century in particular.

Katakana is derived from one part (usually one side) of a kanji, obviously a kanji that had strong associations with a particular sound. Initially there were a range of such kanji for any one given sound, but over time the field narrowed to just one in each case. For example:

ア   (pronounced *a*) derives from the left-hand part β of 阿 .

The reason that the katakana symbol is not graphically identical to the left hand part of the kanji, but is "less squiggly," is because of simplification and stylization. In many cases, there is no modification (other than size) of the chosen part. For example:

力   (pronounced *ka*) derives from the left-hand part 力 of 加 .

Katakana is now used primarily for expressing foreign words (gairaigo), for emphasis, for stylistic reasons, or sometimes for onomatopoeia or mimesis.

Hiragana was associated primarily with women's writing in its early days, and was in fact known as **onnade** ("women's hand"), with men by contrast using full characters or katakana. (Women were not initially en-couraged to write, but it should be noted that in many scholars' opinion the world's first novel is a lengthy "doorstopper" written by a Japanese court lady, Murasaki Shikibu, in 1004, entitled **Genji Monogatari** [*The Tale of Prince Genji*].)

Unlike katakana, hiragana is based on the whole (or virtually the whole) of a kanji, or more exactly the cursive form of that kanji. As with katakana, there were originally a range of kanji that served as phonetic symbols for hiragana, but over time this field too narrowed to one in each case—and not necessarily the same as the one used for katakana. For example, the same **a** and **ka** sounds as above, but this time in hira-gana, are:

あ (pronounced **a**) derives from a cursive rendition of 安 .

か (pronounced **ka**) derives from a cursively simplified 加 .

In this case both the hiragana and katakana **ka** derive from the same kanji. But note how the hiragana **ka** has an extra stroke on the right shoulder, being an (albeit token) inclusion of the right-hand box of the kanji, as opposed to the complete omission of this box in the case of katakana.

The respective meanings of the characters above are "hilly" and "rest-ful" (for **a**) and "add" (for **ka**), but we stress that in the case of kana they are used purely for their sound and not their meaning—just as the En-glish capital letter "A" has nothing to do with the (inverted) original symbol's meaning of "bull's head." We will not provide here a list of all the original kanji.

We do however give you in Table 7a all the kana symbols, using the same schema as for moraic sounds in Part Two. Hiragana is on top, di-rectly below the Roman letters, and katakana is below the hiragana.

TABLE 7a: Kana for basic moraic sounds

	A	I	U	E	O	-YA	-YU	-YO
Vowels	a あ ア	i い イ	u う ウ	e え エ	o お オ			
K-	ka か カ	ki き キ	ku く ク	ke け ケ	ko こ コ	kya きゃ キャ	kyu きゅ キュ	kyo きょ キョ
S-	sa さ サ	shi し シ	su す ス	se せ セ	so そ ソ	sha しゃ シャ	shu しゅ シュ	sho しょ ショ
T-	ta た タ	chi ち チ	tsu つ ツ	te て テ	to と ト	cha ちゃ チャ	chu ちゅ チュ	cho ちょ チョ
N-	na な ナ	ni に ニ	nu ぬ ヌ	ne ね ネ	no の ノ	nya にゃ ニャ	nyu にゅ ニュ	nyo にょ ニョ
H-	ha は ハ	hi ひ ヒ	fu ふ フ	he へ ヘ	ho ほ ホ	hya ひゃ ヒャ	hyu ひゅ ヒュ	hyo ひょ ヒョ
M-	ma ま マ	mi み ミ	mu む ム	me め メ	mo も モ	mya みゃ ミャ	myu みゅ ミュ	myo みょ ミョ
Y-	ya や ヤ		yu ゆ ユ		yo よ ヨ			
R-	ra ら ラ	ri り リ	ru る ル	re れ レ	ro ろ ロ	rya りゃ リャ	ryu りゅ リュ	ryo りょ リョ
W-	wa わ ワ				(o) を ヲ			
-N	-n ん ン							

You will have noticed that in the **-ya**, **-yu**, **-yo** sounds the combination involves writing the **y-** sound with a smaller symbol. Thus きゃ is pronounced **kya** whereas きや would be pronounced **kiya**.

The correspondence between sound and symbol is more consistent in Japanese than in English, but there are three common irregulars: the topic particle **wa** is written は not わ, the object particle **o** is written を not お, and the postposition **e** ("towards") is written へ not え.

The double consonant, as in **issho** ("together"), is made by putting a little つ before the consonant to be doubled, thus いっしょ. The long vowel is formed in the case of long **o** by adding う, or occasionally お. Though **o + o** is often used in texts for all long **o** sounds, the great majority of long **o** sounds are in fact **o + u** rather than **o + o**, and these latter need to be learned case by case. Thus we have そう for **sō** meaning "so," but おおきい for **ōkii** meaning "big." Other common **o + o** words include **tōi** ("far": とおい), **tō** ("ten": とお), and **tōri** ("way" or "road": とおり), plus the latter's verb form **tōru/tōrimasu** meaning "to pass (though)" (とおります). Long **u** takes an extra う, long **a** an extra あ, long **i** an extra い, and long **e** very occasionally an extra え but usually an い, thus おねえさん (elder sister) but せんせい (teacher).

The hardened sounds are shown, as illustrated in Table 7b, by adding two short diacritical strokes on the right shoulder of the appropriate non-hardened symbol. These are known as **dakuten**, meaning literally "voicing/hardening marks." The exception is the semi-hardened **p**, which has a little circle (known as **handakuten**) instead of the strokes.

Whereas hiragana shows a lengthened vowel by simply adding the appropriate **u** or **o**, in the case of foreign words katakana does not normally distinguish and simply uses a lengthening bar ー. Thus "Joe" is written as ジョー, as opposed to the shorter sound in "John," ジョン. However, on the relatively rare occasions when katakana is used of wago or kango, a distinction would normally be made, thus ソウ and オオキイ.

TABLE 7b: Kana for hardened moraic sounds in Japanese

	A	I	U	E	O	-YA	-YU	-YO
G-	ga が ガ	gi ぎ ギ	gu ぐ グ	ge げ ゲ	go ご ゴ	gya ぎゃ ギャ	gyu ぎゅ ギュ	gyo ぎょ ギョ
Z-/J-	za ざ ザ	ji じ ジ	zu ず ズ	ze ぜ ゼ	zo ぞ ゾ	ja じゃ ジャ	ju じゅ ジュ	jo じょ ジョ
D-/J-	da だ ダ	(ji) ぢ ヂ	(zu) づ ヅ	de で デ	do ど ド	(ja) ぢゃ ヂャ	(ju) ぢゅ ヂュ	(jo) ぢょ ヂョ
P-	pa ぱ パ	pi ぴ ピ	pu ぷ プ	pe ぺ ペ	po ぽ ポ	pya ぴゃ ピャ	pyu ぴゅ ピュ	pyo ぴょ ピョ
B-	ba ば バ	bi び ビ	bu ぶ ブ	be べ ベ	bo ぼ ボ	bya びゃ ビャ	byu びゅ ビュ	byo びょ ビョ

The symbols for the "new sounds" in Japanese are shown below in Table 7c. We only give katakana as it would be extremely odd to use hiragana, given the foreign nature of the words prompting these sounds and symbols.

TABLE 7c: Kana for new sounds

	A	I	U	E	O
CH-				cha チェ	
D-		di ディ	du ドゥ		
F-	fa ファ	fi フィ		fe フェ	fo フォ
J-				je ジェ	

	(a)	(i)	(u)	(e)	(o)
SH-				she シェ	
T-		ti ティ	tu トゥ		
V-	va ヴァ	vi ヴィ	vu ヴ	ve ヴェ	vo ヴォ
W-		wi ウィ		we ウェ	wo ウォ

You will have seen that the new sound combinations borrow the same principle as with the *-ya* sounds, in that the second symbol is written smaller to indicate a contraction of the two moras into one, with the vowel sound of the first mora largely disappearing. This time, however, straight vowels rather than *y-* sounds are used for the second sound.

It is in fact possible to follow this principle to make up still more sounds as and when necessary. For example, ***kwo*** could be expressed by クォ.

No kana symbol has more than four strokes, but like kanji, they must be written in a standard stroke order and stroke direction. There are two golden rules to follow:

1) Top to bottom   2) Left to right

That is, the top left corner (if there is one) is the normal place to start.

In the case of ***a*/ あ/ ア** for example:

一   ナ   あ   and   フ   ア

Another way of showing the order, used in many introductory textbooks, is to give numbers, usually at the head of each stroke (thereby removing the need for arrows too, which are also used in some textbooks). Thus:

あ and ア . We give you a full list below in Table 7d.

TABLE 7d: Kana stroke order

あ ア	い イ	う ウ	え エ	お オ
か カ	き キ	く ク	け ケ	こ コ
さ サ	し シ	す ス	せ セ	そ ソ
た タ	ち チ	つ ツ	て テ	と ト
な ナ	に ニ	ぬ ヌ	ね ネ	の ノ
は ハ	ひ ヒ	ふ フ	へ ヘ	ほ ホ
ま マ	み ミ	む ム	め メ	も モ
や ヤ		ゆ ユ		よ ヨ
ら ラ	り リ	る ル	れ レ	ろ ロ
わ ワ				を ヲ
ん ン				

(This is a font that clearly separates strokes, e.g. き rather than the more cursive き. You need to be familiar with a range of graphic styles.)

Kana that are used to follow kanji, so as to show a variable ending, are called *okurigana* (literally "sending off kana"). Thus, in for example the case of *kaimasu* ("to buy"), this would be written 買います. The kanji means "buy" and is pronounced here as *ka*, representing the unchanging stem. The *okurigana* add the *i*, *ma*, and *su*. The kanji itself is neither negative nor affirmative, and is also without tense. To express "didn't buy," i.e. *kaimasen deshita*, this would be 買いませんでした。 (Notice how we have used a Japanese full-stop here: it is hollow.)

The term *okurigana* should not be confused with *furigana* ("added kana"), which are used to show the pronunciation of a kanji. Lines of Japanese script can be written either horizontally (left to right) or vertically (top to bottom, from the right), so *furigana* would be used respectively on top of a kanji (or very occasionally underneath it) or on its right-hand side, necessarily being written small. A more convenient method that has evolved over the years is to put the *furigana* in brackets, and to write them in normal size (though they can also be written smaller). This is less strain on the eyes (and less demanding of word-processing skills!), and tends to be the system used in newspapers, but it does have its critics from an aesthetic perspective.

As an example of typical *furigana*, using obscure kanji meaning "parrot," we could write "I bought a parrot" (hopefully not a dead one!)—
Ōmu o kaimashita—as either:

鸚鵡（おおむ）を買いました。 or 鸚鵡を買いました。

Furigana (either in smaller gloss or in brackets) are not commonly used except in the case of children's texts or obscure kanji, and in those cases where newspapers use kanji outside the range officially prescribed. (More on the latter in 7.1.3.) Novelists also sometimes use *furigana* stylistically in combination with an unorthodox kanji for a given word in order to give a particular nuance to that word, such as for example using a kanji meaning "imagine" and giving it the *furigana* おも plus okurigana います to represent **omoimasu** meaning "to think."

Logically, it would be the height of absurdity if *furigana* had to be used extensively as a matter of course, as it would mean that the kanji by themselves were ineffective and that the whole writing system was unnecessarily time-consuming!

Finally, you may occasionally encounter (especially in vertical writing) a repetition sign ゝ. Thus ききます could be written きゝます. If the repeated kana sign is the hardened version, then you can use the sign ゞ. Thus はば ("width") could be written はゞ. There is also a sign for repeating two syllables (as e.g. in **iroiro**), used only in vertical script, which is like a thin 〱 (or 〲) occupying two vertical spaces. The use of these various signs, which are not so common nowadays, is optional.

7.1.3 Kanji

As mentioned earlier, the word "kanji" literally means "symbol from Han China," clearly indicating the Chinese origin of these characters. The earliest origins go back to about 2,000–1,500 BC, in the Yellow River region.

There are about 3,000 kanji from this early period, though the number had grown to around 50,000 by AD 200—that is, there are more kanji in existence than most people's entire stock of words! This was still centuries before the Japanese started adopting them, so they were in a sense spoiled for choice. Though theoretically any one of more than 60,000 kanji might appear in older Japanese texts, in practice no more than a tenth of these were actually used with any frequency, and nowadays you will find only around 2,000 in common use.

One reason for this reduction was a series of reforms, especially in the postwar period. Shortly after the end of World War Two the Occupation forces instigated, through the Ministry of Education, a major reform that limited the kanji for use in official publications to 1,850 (plus a further 92 for use in proper nouns). These were called the **Tōyō Kanji** (literally "Temporary Use Kanji"). Of these 1,850 kanji, 881 were designated for learning progressively during the six grades of elementary school. These 881 were commonly known as **Kyōiku Kanji**, meaning literally "Educational Kanji," also known in English as "Essential Kanji."

In 1981 another major reform took place, in which the corpus of kanji was increased to 1,945, of which 996 were Kyōiku Kanji. The overall corpus was renamed **Jōyō Kanji**, meaning "General Use Kanji." A slight modification occurred in 1989, which saw the number of Kyōiku Kanji increased to 1,006, though the overall corpus remained at 1,945 and retained the same name Jōyō Kanji. (The breakdown per grade for the Kyōiku Kanji is Grade One: 80, Grade Two: 160, Grade Three: 200, Grade Four: 200, Grade Five: 185, and Grade Six: 181.) The number of additional characters approved for proper nouns has now increased to 285.

In 2001 the Japan Newspaper Association recommended that a further 39 (common noun) kanji should be treated as not requiring furigana in its publications, so in line with this there may well be a further change to the Jōyō Kanji in the not-too-distant future.

Thus there has been a trend towards a slight expansion of kanji in recent decades relative to the somewhat drastic simplification of the Occupation Period, this recent expansion probably being helped by the advent of word-processors. It is also probably true to say that the use of word-processors has meant that the ability to recognize kanji has become even more important relative to the ability to write them.

The stroke count for the Jōyō Kanji varies from a simple one (as in 一, meaning "one") to 23 (as in 鑑, meaning "model"), with the average being 10.3 strokes. Almost exactly half the Jōyō Kanji fall within the stroke range 8–12.

Most kanji (60%) have two types of pronunciation or "reading": the **on** (literally "sound") reading, which is based on the original Chinese pronunciation, and the **kun** (literally "taught") reading, which is based on the native Japanese reading. Some kanji have multiple readings both in *on* and *kun*, while others might have only one single reading, either just one *on* or *kun*. In textbooks that introduce kanji, *on* readings are usually Romanized in upper case or written in katakana, *kun* in lower case or hiragana. It is often the case—but by no means always—that compound words of multiple kanji use *on* readings while single words consisting of a single kanji use *kun*.

Statistically, the 1,945 Jōyō Kanji have an average of 1.12 *on* readings and 0.84 *kun* readings, though it is by no means the case that the vast majority neatly have one *on* and one *kun*. The kanji 生, for example, has six distinct *kun* readings spanning meanings such as "life," "birth," "raw," "growth," "plants" and "pure" (and a mere two *on*).

As a detailed example of a common and slightly tricky kanji, the kanji for **ikimasu** ("to go"), 行, has the *on* readings **KŌ**, **GYŌ**, and, rarely, **AN**; and it also has *kun* readings **i-** (as in the stem of **ikimasu**), **yu-** (as in the older pronunciation of **ikimasu**, namely **yukimasu**), and **okona-** (as in the verb **okonaimasu** meaning "to carry out": some texts give just **oko-**).

The reason it has three *on* readings reflects changes in pronunciation in time and place in ancient China, with each of the kanji's multiple pronunciations entering Japan, probably at different times. As a common character with a broad core meaning, it has also diversified semantically, being used in its original Chinese setting to express in writing two different but related concepts of "to go" and "to act"/"carry out," and being consequently applied to two native Japanese words with those meanings. It also has, both in Chinese and Japanese, the idea of "column," or "line" (of text). In the latter case it is almost always pronounced **GYŌ** (as in **gyōretsu** 行列 meaning a "queue" and **ichigyōme** 一行目 meaning the "first line of text"). The reading **KŌ**, by contrast, is associated with "going" (as in **ryokō** 旅行 meaning a "journey") or "acting" (as in **kōi** 行為 meaning "an action"). **AN** also means "go," but is only nowadays found in a few old words such as **angya** 行脚, meaning "pilgrimage". It is not always the case that different *on* readings are so helpfully associated with different meanings!

Sometimes a Chinese meaning is lost in Japanese. For example, the **ryo** 旅 of the above word **ryokō** 旅行 meaning a "journey" also means "journey" by itself in Japanese, with a *kun* reading **tabi**, but in Chinese it still very occasionally has an old and more literal meaning of a "cohort of soldiers" (the kanji being derived from an ideograph showing a group of people gathered under a streaming banner). This is not so in Japanese.

Conversely, sometimes a meaning is added or changed in Japanese. For example, the kanji **YŌ** 曜 means "dazzling" or "bird plumage" in Chinese but in Japanese hardly ever has these meanings. Instead, it has a meaning of "day of the week" (as in 土曜日 **doyōbi** meaning "Saturday"), which is completely lacking in Chinese.

In a handful of cases, the Japanese have made up their own kanji, known as **kokuji** ("national kanji"). For example, the Japanese took the Chinese kanji for "to move," 動, and added an element 亻, meaning "person," to produce 働, meaning "person moving," which was used to indicate "work." This was subsequently "reverse-imported" into Chinese, which originally used only the character 労 for "work": this latter character is also used in Japanese but tends to have a meaning rather of heavier and/or organized "labor."

The above element 亻 is one of 214 traditional semantic elements known as radicals, of which about 40 are used particularly commonly. Other common radicals include 月 for "meat"/"body," and 木 for "tree"/"wood." They give a rough idea of what general area of meaning a kanji will have. Usually radicals are on the left side of a kanji or above it, but sometimes below, and occasionally on the right side. This sounds confusing but you do quite quickly become familiar with them.

The radicals are often (but not always) simple kanji in themselves (when written larger). For example, 木 is read *ki* in *kun*, and is a stand-alone word meaning "tree," whereas in compounds it usually has one of its *on* readings *MOKU* or—less commonly—*BOKU*, as e.g. *zaimoku* 材木 meaning "timber" or *taiboku* 大木 meaning "large tree."

The kanji 木 is a pictograph, clearly representing a tree with its upright trunk and sweeping branches, and this is one of six traditional character types as given below (though, as will become clear presently, it can be argued that there are really only four distinct types).

There is some vagueness and overlap in category ascription, so these should only be treated as rough guides—and in any event, knowledge of categories is not important for actual use of kanji, and is given here only for information and interest. They are:

1. The pictograph: this is basically a picture of a physical object. In addition to tree 木, we could give 田 (*DEN*, *ta*), showing and meaning "paddy field." Some have become considerably stylized, as shown in Figure 7a.

FIGURE 7a: Some pictographic origins

女 woman: from kneeling stick-figure

馬 horse: from rotated stick-figure 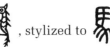, stylized to

目 eye: angularized from rotated picture

子 child: from wrapped infant showing arms

山 mountain: from mountain range

2. The sign or symbol: This is essentially the abstract equivalent of a pictograph. A clear example is 回 (***KAI, mawa*[*ru*]** [v.i.] / ***mawa*[*su*]** [v.t.]), meaning "to turn," which is the angularised form of a curved vortex symbolizing spinning/turning as shown in Figure 7b. We also give the origins of a few other example symbols.

FIGURE 7b: Some symbolic origins

回 turn/spin: angularized from spinning vortex

上 above/top: from symbol indicating above

下 below/bottom: from symbol indicating below

中 center/middle: from flagpole with central and outer shafts

3. The ideograph: This type of kanji is a combination of pictographs and/or symbols to convey another idea. For example, putting two trees 木 together gives 林 (***RIN, hayashi***), meaning "forest" (suggestive of fairly tall and stately trees), while putting three together gives 森 (***SHIN, mori***), meaning "woods" (suggestive of more but less stately trees).

As another particularly clear example, using one of the handful of kokuji, we can consider 峠 (***tōge***). This is composed of three characters in their own right, 山 (***SAN, yama***), meaning "hill" or "mountain," plus two kanji from Figure 7b, 上, here meaning "up," and 下, here meaning "down," to give a very logical meaning of "mountain pass" or "crest," with an extended meaning of "crisis."

4. The phonetic-ideograph or semasio-phonetic. This category accounts for more than 85% of all kanji, but it is also particularly "fuzzy." In essence it is a combination of an element of meaning (i.e. semantic) with an element of sound (i.e. phonetic), but in actual fact in many cases the phonetic elements also have a semantic role too, meaning that such kanji can also be considered ideographs as well. That is, where there is a range of kanji that could be used to express a given sound, it makes sense that the one that is chosen also has a semantic relevance. For example, let us consider the kanji 注, which once had an *on* reading **SHU** but is now read **CHŪ**, a *kun* reading **soso(gu)**, and a meaning of "to pour." It comprises a semantic radical 氵, meaning "water"/"liquid," and a kanji 主. The latter plays a phonetic role, for it too is pronounced **SHU** in its *on* reading. Its pronunciation in ancient times was the same as that of a more complex character meaning "continuous," so it was chosen to represent that sound and give the idea of "continuous liquid," i.e "flowing" or "pouring." Nowadays 主 means "master" or "owner" or by extension "principal," but this meaning is derived in fact from a pictograph of a tall-stemmed burning oil lamp, which was symbolically lit (or ordered to be lit) by the master of the house. Thus the kanji has strong associations with the idea of something being long and upright, which strengthens the idea of pouring liquid thanks to its image of a column of liquid.

Interestingly, if the water radical is replaced by the wood radical, giving 柱, then the meaning becomes not a column of liquid but a column of wood, i.e. a pillar. This is in fact the meaning of 柱, which similarly had an *on* reading of **SHU** that has now become **CHŪ** (and a *kun* reading of **hashira**).

The fact that the reading **SHU** has been dropped in the case of 注 and 柱 but not 主 shows how complex it can be to research these matters.

Traditionally the semasio-phonetic category has treated the main role of the non-radical element as being a phonetic one, with any semantic role being treated as secondary, but there are not a few cases where the opposite might be argued—i.e. that the semantic element is the more important and the phonetic role secondary. An example might be the character for "blind" 盲, which has a *kun* reading **mekura** and *on* readings **BŌ** and **MŌ**. It comprises the kanji 亡, meaning "to die" with a *kun* reading of

na(kunaru) and *on* readings ***BŌ***, and ***MŌ***, along with the kanji 目 meaning "eye" (***MOKU, me***). Clearly 亡 plays a phonetic role, but is this in
fact the primary role? Is it not more a case of it acting primarily in a semantic role, to express "dead eyes," with the phonetic role being merely
secondary and confined to *on* readings in compounds? In other words, is
it a semasio-phonetic, or an ideograph, and of course the answer is that it
is both. This shows the danger of any inflexible categorization.

As was the case with 柱 above, if 亡 is combined with another radical,
this time 心 (***SHIN, kokoro***), meaning "heart" or "mind," then we get
忘 (***BŌ, wasu[reru]***), meaning "to forget," which is clearly semantically
related to the idea of a "dead mind."

Not all semasio-phonetic kanji show quite such consistency and clarity
in their phonetic or semantic evolution, but the principle is the same. In
short, the category should be considered as one in which elements are
combined for, in most cases, both semantic and phonetic reasons in
order to express in writing an extended concept. It is often a "line-call"
as to whether the phonetic or semantic role of the non-radical element
has priority.

5. Characters of changed meaning or pronunciation: This is a somewhat
vague category, since some scholars apply it only to kanji whose original
meaning has been completely lost, and others to kanji which have simply developed extended meanings. It is also taxonomically different from
the preceding four since it relates to usage rather than origin per se and
necessarily comprises characters from other categories. A good example
within the stricter definition is the kanji for "east," 東 (***TŌ, higashi***),
which is usually interpreted as an ideograph comprising the sun 日 rising behind a tree 木, thus indicating sunrise and hence the east (though
theoretically it could be argued equally that it represents the setting sun
and hence the west). In fact, although this interpretation is a useful
mnemonic and has been in existence for at least a thousand years, it is
incorrect. Very early forms show it to be a pictograph depicting a large
trussed bundle with a pole through it (the "branches" being ends of
rope), and it is actually closely related to the character 束 (***SOKU, taba***),
which means "bundle" and can etymologically be considered a variant
form of 東. However, for whatever reason—possibly a phonetic borrowing, but possibly even a simple mistake by someone in high office whom

nobody dared correct—東 was used to express "east," and no longer means "bundle."

There are a surprising number of kanji that have been borrowed or mis-used in this fashion over the centuries, indeed as many as 15% of the Jōyō Kanji.

6. Phonetically borrowed characters: This is often confused with the previous category, and similarly relates to usage rather than origin, but it has a focus exclusively on pronunciation, with meaning not being an issue. Kanji in this bracket are, rather like the kanji used to produce kana, used in effect just for their sound in certain situations. For exam-ple, the proper noun "America" can be expressed with the four kanji 亜米利加, with respective pronunciations of **a-me(i)-ri-ka**, or "France" as 仏蘭西 (**fu[tsu]-ran-se[i]**). In some cases one of the kanji in the name, usually the first, is used by itself as a symbol of that country. Thus 仏 can be used to indicate France.

The use of kanji in this way is not common apart from in the case of names of places, or of course people. Foreigners can have great fun try-ing to work out a kanji version of their names, and will find their Japanese friends very enthusiastic in trying to come up with appropriate suggestions. The female name Carol, for example, can be written with the kanji 佳露瑠, (**ka-ro-ru**) meaning respectively "beautiful," "dew" and "jewel"—a delightful poetic rendition. But the tragedy is that you also need to be humble, so those of you called Carol couldn't actually let it be known that you'd come up with this yourself as it would be considered conceited! (You should never imply that you think yourself beautiful.) Better to drop hints to an appropriate Japanese (male) friend so that he can be given credit for devising it, while you modestly add of course how inappropriate it is.

As the above might suggest, kanji can be fun at times. And they can also be valuable insights into the way concepts evolve as a reflection of the way the world has been ordered and interpreted in a given time and place, albeit that this is usually China of several millennia ago and hence is some considerable way removed from modern Japan. As in most of the ancient world, life in the birth place of kanji was not always delicate and refined. Reference to slaves, for example, is very common in the etymology of kanji. Among other things in this regard, the origin of the kanji for **boku** meaning "I"/"me," 僕, is actually derived from a complex ideograph showing a slave carrying a chamber-pot complete with graphically depicted contents!

We will not give you here any lists of kanji for you to learn, for we recommend that you acquire a specialist kanji book, one that gives you full sets of readings and meanings, and, if you are interested, also their origins.

Instead, with a combined aim of revision and exposure to Japanese script, we give in 7.2 some of the sentences we have used in Romanization in Part Three to illustrate grammar points.

We will however first give a few sample illustrations, in Figure 7c, of the fact that kanji too, like kana, need to be written in a given stroke order (which similarly usually follows the rules of and top to bottom and left to right). Among other things, this is important when strokes are joined and/or simplified, as in many hand-written letters.

The extreme in this regard is the famous highly cursive **sōsho** or "grass script" of classical Japanese, as seen for example in old scrolls in museums. This is still occasionally encountered today in certain formal or artistic circumstances but it is extremely difficult to read, far more so than say Elizabethan script in English. Moreover it is only produced by brush, or occasionally pen, not print. In fact, sōsho is beyond the abilities of many native speakers even to read, let alone write, and as foreigners you would never be expected to use it except perhaps in a specialist calligraphy classroom. We will therefore not introduce it here, but would recommend anyone interested to approach a calligraphy teacher.

FIGURE 7c: Illustration of kanji stroke order

(These are the three kanji comprising **Nihongo**, the Japanese language.)

Stroke order is also important for stroke count. Kanji dictionaries have traditionally used a look-up method based on "radical plus remaining strokes," which is still in fact very useful if you don't know a single reading for the character you are looking up. Thus **go** 語 above would be the speech radical 言, itself listed under "7 stroke radicals" (but which would soon become familiar to students as Radical #149 under the traditional sequencing system for the 214 radicals), plus seven additional strokes—i.e. "7 + 7" or "149 + 7." It's particularly important here to note that the box part 口 of both the radical 言 and of the remaining strokes 吾 is three strokes, not four, as the top and right-hand lines are written as one stroke.

If you don't know the radical, depending on the dictionary you can also simply count the total strokes, and for example look 語 up under "14 strokes."

However, as we have said earlier, usually the quickest look-up method is to use the readings index if you happen to know a reading (and, of course, if a readings index is provided!).

Finally, a reminder that if you forget a kanji, you can always use kana. It is recognition that is more important.

7.2 Japanese script versions of review sentences

Japanese script nowadays can be written either horizontally left to right (though in historical times right to left was also used), or vertically top to bottom (from the right). Fiction tends to be written vertically, non-fiction as either vertical or horizontal. Newspapers and magazines have a mixture of both, with the main body of text usually being vertical but photo captions and other text horizontal. Adverts often contain both vertical and horizontal text within the same ad. Most publications with predominantly vertical script open from left to right, in the opposite way to that in the West, whereas those with predominantly horizontal script follow the Western way, but be prepared for exceptions. Thus navigating your way around a Japanese publication, especially a newspaper, is not always a simple matter!

There are also a few "fiddly" related conventions, such as with numbers, where in general the kanji for numbers are used in vertical script, but (with a few exceptions), digits for horizontal script.

As we will be using *furigana* here (for all kanji) in these review sentences, for convenience we use horizontal script.

You will also note that, whatever the orientation of the script, there is no spacing between words. Word breaks are only found in children's material, and are in any case different from what English speakers might expect, with for example **watashi wa** わたしは as in the sentence below grouped together as one unit, and similarly **tegami o** てがみを. That is, particles are treated as part of the word they follow. We follow the "no word-break" practice here as this is more natural.

Nor does Japanese script have any provision for the equivalent of capital letters in Romanization, and it is also very rare to see bold or italic print. It does however have a range of punctuation marks—fewer than English, though English punctuation is being increasingly used in horizontal script. Note the commas, full stops, and occasional quotation marks in the sentences that follow, but also observe that the question mark and exclamation mark are not used in "orthodox" Japanese.

The repetition sign for kanji is 々, so **wareware** (meaning "we") could be written 我々. It is used rather more frequently than the kana repetition sign.

So, let us move on to the sentences. We may vary these very slightly.

私は手紙を書きません。
Watashi wa tegami o kakimasen.
I don't write letters./I won't write a letter.

だれが書きますか。
Dare ga kakimasu ka.
Who'll write it?

私が書きます。
Watashi ga kakimasu.
I'll write it.

友達は雑誌は読みますけれども、本は読みません。
Tomodachi wa zasshi wa yomimasu keredomo, hon wa yomimasen.
My friend reads magazines but doesn't read books.

ジョンさんの手紙を読みませんでした。
Jon-san no tegami o yomimasen deshita.
I didn't read John's letter.

イギリス人のジョンさんは日本語の本を読みました。
Igirisujin no Jon-san wa Nihongo no hon o yomimashita.
John, the/an Englishman, read a Japanese book.

ジョンさんの妹さんの日本人のボーイフレンドは「私は何も書きませんでした」と言いました。
Jon-san no imōtosan no Nihonjin no bōifurendo wa "Watashi wa nanimo kakimasen deshita" to iimashita.
The Japanese boyfriend of John's younger sister said, "I didn't write anything." (Note quote marks.)

マイクさんは先生ではありません。
Maiku-san wa sensei de wa arimasen.
Mike is not a/the teacher.

犬は部屋にいませんでした。
Inu wa heya ni imasen deshita.
The dog wasn't in the room.

パリはフランスにあります。
Pari wa Furansu ni arimasu.
Paris is in France.

箱の中には何がありますか。
Hako no naka ni wa nani ga arimasu ka.
What's inside the box?

メアリーさんは友達と一緒に映画館に行きました。
Mearii-san wa tomodachi to issho ni eigakan ni ikimashita.
Mary went to the cinema with a friend.

宿題を終わりましたから、テレビを見ます。
Shukudai o owarimashita kara, terebi o mimasu.
I've finished my homework so I'll watch TV.

あの山<ruby>山<rt>やま</rt></ruby>は高<ruby>高<rt>たか</rt></ruby>いです。
Ano yama wa takai desu.
That mountain is tall.

そのスカートはきれいですねえ。高<ruby>高<rt>たか</rt></ruby>かったですか。
Sono sukāto wa kirei desu nē. Takakatta desu ka.
That skirt's pretty. Was it expensive?

サーフィンはそんなに難<ruby>難<rt>むず</rt></ruby>かしくありません。
Sāfin wa sonna ni muzukashiku arimasen.
Surfing isn't all that difficult.

りんごを三<ruby>三<rt>み</rt></ruby>つ買<ruby>買<rt>か</rt></ruby>いました。
Ringo o mittsu kaimashita.
I bought three apples.

3 週間<ruby>週間<rt>しゅうかん</rt></ruby>働<ruby>働<rt>はたら</rt></ruby>きました。
Sanshūkan hatarakimashita.
I worked for three weeks. (Digits are used in horizontal writing except for numbers ending in *-tsu*.)

本<ruby>本<rt>ほん</rt></ruby>を買<ruby>買<rt>か</rt></ruby>った男<ruby>男<rt>おとこ</rt></ruby>の人<ruby>人<rt>ひと</rt></ruby>はアメリカ人<ruby>人<rt>じん</rt></ruby>です。
Hon o katta otoko no hito wa Amerikajin desu.
The man who bought the book is an American.

あした行<ruby>行<rt>い</rt></ruby>くつもりです。
Ashita iku tsumori desu.
I intend to go tomorrow.

今日<ruby>今日<rt>きょう</rt></ruby>行<ruby>行<rt>い</rt></ruby>かない訳<ruby>訳<rt>わけ</rt></ruby>ですか。
Kyō ikanai wake desu ka.
Does this mean you're not going today?

買<ruby>買<rt>か</rt></ruby>ったのはよかったです。／買<ruby>買<rt>か</rt></ruby>ってよかったです。
Katta no wa yokatta desu.
It was good that I bought it./The one I bought was good. (Out of context, *Katte yokatta desu*—literally "buying was good"—is less ambiguous for "It was good that I bought it.")

パリへ行ったことがありますか。
Pari e itta koto ga arimasu ka.
Have you ever been to Paris?

今の学生があまり宿題をしないということは問題です。
Ima no gakusei ga amari shukudai o shinai to iu koto wa mondai desu.
The fact (that) students don't do much homework nowadays is a problem.

去年から勉強しています。
Kyonen kara benkyō shite imasu.
I have been studying since last year.

私の本をもう読みましたか。 いえ、 まだ読んでいません。
Watashi no hon o mō yomimashita ka. Ie, mada yonde imasen.
Have you read my book yet? No, I haven't read it yet.

友達にペンを貸してあげました。
Tomodachi ni pen o kashite agemashita.
I lent my friend a pen.

先生は日本語の文法を説明して下さいました。
Sensei wa Nihongo no bunpō o setsumei shite kudasaimashita.
The teacher explained Japanese grammar (to/for me).

お名前を書いて下さい。
O-namae o kaite kudasai.
Please write your name.

行ってもいいですか。
Itte mo ii desu ka.
May I go?

メアリーさんは5時に来て、 6時にうちに帰りました。
Mearii-san wa goji ni kite, rokuji ni uchi ni kaerimashita.
Mary came at five o'clock and went home at six.

非常に暑くて、 いやな天気でした。
Hijō ni atsukute, iya na tenki deshita.
It was extremely hot and unpleasant weather.

何も言わないで下さい。
Nanimo iwanaide kudasai.
Please don't say anything.

行きましょうか。
Ikimashō ka.
Shall we go?

読もうとしましたけれども、字が小さくて、だめでした。
Yomō to shimashita keredomo, ji ga chiisakute, dame deshita.
I tried to read (it), but the print was too small and (so) it was hopeless.

読んでみましたけれども、あまり面白くありませんでした。
Yonde mimashita keredomo, amari omoshiroku arimasen deshita.
I tried reading (it) but it wasn't very interesting.

宏さんは学生でしょう。
Hiroshi-san wa gakusei deshō.
Hiroshi's probably a student.

先生は行かないかもしれません。
Sensei wa ikanai ka mo shiremasen.
The teacher might not go.

難しかったら、しなくてもいいですよ。
Muzukashikattara, shinakute mo ii desu yo.
If it's difficult, you don't have to do it.

日本語を勉強したいなら、まずこの本を読んで下さい。
Nihongo o benkyō shitai nara, mazu kono hon o yonde kudasai.
If you're wanting to study Japanese, please read this book first. (***mazu*** means "first of all")

これを読めば分かります。
Kore o yomeba wakarimasu.
If you read this then you'll understand.

これを読まなければなりません。
Kore o yomanakereba narimasen.
You must read this.

それを食べてはいけません。
Sore o tabete wa ikemasen.
You mustn't eat that.

雨が降ると、テニスをしません。
Ame ga furu to, tenisu o shimasen.
We don't play tennis if/when(ever) it rains.

マイクさんは昨日来たようです。
Maiku-san wa kinō kita yō desu.
It seems/looks like Mike came yesterday.

そうみたいです。
Sō mitai desu.
It looks that way.

アフリカは暑いそうです。
Afurika wa atsui sō desu.
They say that Africa's hot.

アフリカは暑そうです。
Afurika wa atsusō desu.
Africa looks like it's hot.

先生になるために日本語を勉強しています。
Sensei ni naru tame ni Nihongo o benkyō shite imasu.
I'm studying Japanese (in order) to become a teacher.

面接がうまくいくように準備しています。
Mensetsu ga umaku iku yō ni junbi shite imasu.
I'm preparing so that my interview will go well.

雨が降っていたので、行きませんでした。
Ame ga futte ita no de, ikimasen deshita.
It was raining so I didn't go.

オレンジとりんごとでは、どちらの方が安いですか。
Orenji to ringo to (de wa), dochira no hō ga yasui desu ka.
Which is the cheaper, oranges or apples?

スペインはアイスランドより暑いです。
Supein wa Aisurando yori atsui desu.
Spain is hotter than Iceland.

行かない方がいいです。
Ikanai hō ga ii desu.
It's better not to go.

どうしたらいいか分かりません。
Dō shitara ii ka wakarimasen.
I don't know what I should do.

林 先生と話してみたらどうですか。
Hayashi-sensei to hanashite mitara dō desu ka.
What about if you tried talking to Professor Hayashi?

私にはこんな仕事は出来ません。
Watashi (ni) wa konna shigoto wa dekimasen.
I can't do this sort of work.

私は日本語が話せます。
Watashi wa Nihongo ga hanasemasu.
I can speak Japanese.

これは広く知られています。
Kore wa hiroku shirarete imasu.
This is widely known.

お金を盗まれました。
O-kane o nusumaremashita.
I had my money stolen.

窓は開けてあります。
Mado wa akete arimasu.
The window has been opened.

先生は学生に漢字を書かせました。
Sensei wa gakusei ni kanji o kakasemashita.
The teacher made/let the students write kanji.

読ませて頂けないでしょうか。
Yomasete itadakenai deshō ka.
Could I possibly be allowed to read it?

日本語を習いたいです。
Nihongo ga naraitai desu.
I want to learn Japanese.

運転しながらラジオを聞いていました。
Unten shinagara rajio o kiite imashita.
I was listening to the radio as I was driving.

猫が寝ている間にねずみが逃げました。
Neko ga nete iru aida ni nezumi ga nigemashita.
The mouse escaped while the cat slept.

食べる前に手を洗いましょう。
Taberu mae ni te o araimashō.
Let's wash our hands before we eat.

宿題を終わってからテレビを見ました。
Shukudai o owatte kara terebi o mimashita.
I watched TV after finishing my homework.

これしか出来ませんでした。
Kore shika dekimasen deshita.
This was all I could manage.

行くかどうか分かりません。
Iku ka dō ka wakarimasen.
I don't know if I'll go or not.

漢字を勉強してみたら、どんなに覚えにくいかすぐ分かると思います。

Kanji o benkyō shite mitara, donna ni oboenikui ka sugu wakaru to omoimasu.

If you try studying kanji, I think you'll soon appreciate just how difficult they are to remember.

Actually, we don't want to end on such a negative note, even though it's a good grammatical illustration, so let's change that last one to:

日本語を勉強してみたら、どんなに面白くて楽しいかすぐ分かると思います。

Nihongo o benkyō shite mitara, donna ni omoshirokute tanoshii ka sugu wakaru to omoimasu.

If you try studying Japanese, I think you'll soon appreciate just how interesting and enjoyable it is.

This concludes our section on the writing system. As you will have seen, it is a fascinating script, and certainly it has its challenges. Time is one of the most demanding factors when it comes to mastering the kanji. But don't forget our earlier advice, that you can get by in the initial stages by using kana to express yourself, while you concentrate on recognizing as many kanji as you can. Actively writing kanji yourself can normally—outside the relatively artificial setting of a classroom—be given a lesser priority, especially in the current age when word-processors are so widely used. But having said that, it is fun to try writing kanji yourself, and we by no means suggest you should ignore this.

Good luck.

Afterword

We hope that you have enjoyed working through our introductory description of the Japanese language, that you have now come to feel a sense of familiarity with the language, and that you want to continue to learn more about it.

We will not name specific titles here, but we recommend that you equip yourself with:

- a Japanese-English dictionary that gives illustrative sentences
- an English-Japanese dictionary that gives kana readings as well as kanji and also gives illustrative sentences
- a self-study textbook that takes you through to an advanced stage in grammar (and includes pitch accents)
- a specialist book on kana and kanji usage
- a kanji dictionary with an easy look-up system and a readings index
- a book on the origins of kanji (one that gives authentic origins, not assumed origins based on current graphic forms)

And of course, we recommend that you cultivate a wide network of native Japanese friends and acquaintances, and use Japanese as much as possible in as wide a variety of situations as possible. Don't be proud, and ask for help and correction (though not to the point of boring your friends silly!). Enroll in suitable courses if these are available. And naturally, actually going to Japan is a great plus, especially if you have developed a language platform before going there as this will enable you to make the most linguistically out of the trip.

Don't forget that a good language speaker should also have a good working knowledge of the relevant culture and society and history, so we also recommend that, if you don't already have such knowledge, you spend some time reading up. This too is a case where a good platform of knowledge before going to Japan can be especially helpful.

But above all, ENJOY.

Perhaps
I'll see you
around!